IT'S THE CITIES,
STUPID!

DR. MIKE DUFFY

IT'S THE CITIES, STUPID!

CITY-DWELLERS, BEWARE!

ISBN 979-8-9894314-1-0 (paperback)
ISBN 979-8-9894314-2-7 (e-book)

All Scripture is taken from the AUTHORIZED KING JAMES VERSION.

Editing by Gretchen Doolittle
Cover design and typesetting by Jenneth Dyck

TABLE OF CONTENTS

INTRODUCTION

As the crowd of more than a thousand sat stunned and speechless, the veteran missionary of more than 40 years told of his exploits in South America. Dr. Ernest Gambrell hoped that by sharing the work that God had done in his life over the past fruitful decades, that God would draw others to surrender their lives and step up to continue the work in the region that he was about to leave. He shared stories of tragedy and difficulty that would break the heart of any compassionate listener. He testified of the amazing grace of God, changing for the better the lives of the native peoples in remote villages, isolated deep in the jungles of the Amazon.

What I remembered most about the message he shared that night was the description he gave of a beautiful painting that he had seen with his own eyes. As I remember, he said the picture was titled "Eternity." Dr. Gambrell described the stunning picture as being a beautiful mural painting stretching wall to wall. It was at the end of the room opposite from where he was standing. In the painting, there was a high cliff that seemed to run the entire width of the picture. At the top of the cliff were lines of people, multitudes of people, and each line marching single file toward the cliff's edge.

The picture projected motion, depicting the people in the front of each line taking a step, going over the cliff, and falling into the fiery abyss of hell, which would be their eternal dwelling place. The flames aggressively extended out of the bottom of the chasm, reaching out in expectation of seizing their next victim. Gambrell said he was so moved by the images that he began to cry. He stood there for what seemed to be a long time, gazing at the horrible sight. It troubled his soul. One haunting question kept cycling through his mind: "Why would a person take that last step?"

With no clear answer and weary from standing there and contemplating, he began to walk toward the scene. As he drew closer to the picture, the answer became obvious. Gambrell said that when he got close enough to see the detail of the painting, he could see the eyes of the people who were marching. They were blind! They had no idea the edge of the cliff was there! They did not realize they were taking their final step of life and tumbling to their fiery fate. To Gambrell's perceptive eyes, it seemed as though they had no reason to think they were in immediate peril. The reality was, however, their immediate future held nothing but danger and destruction. One heartbeat, one step away from eternal disaster! They were now past the point of no return!

And so it seems today, far too many voters ignorantly go about life, and then with blind allegiance, they cast their vote. And once cast, they too are beyond the point of no return. They stepped over the cliff's edge. There are no "do-overs" in this process. Unfortunately, forethought and consideration are rarely given to the consequences of that vote. They are ignorant, even sometimes "willingly ignorant," of the trouble they are bringing upon themselves by following the deceitful charlatans they adore and admire so much!

If only someone could get the voters to stop and think before casting their votes! If one could persuade the citizen to listen to the "truth, the whole truth, and nothing but the truth," before making their decision. If they could be taught and challenged "how to think," instead of "what to think," maybe the tide of low-information voters could be turned to logic and reason.

IT'S THE ECONOMY, STUPID! OR IS IT?

It seems as though every election cycle the political pundits reduce their agendas to one simple issue that will have the greatest influence on the outcome of the elections—the economy. The catchy little phrase "It's the economy, stupid" has become standard fare for the opinion writers and the politicians.

> "The economy, stupid" is a phrase that was coined by James Carville in 1992. It is often quoted from a televised quip by Carville as "It's the economy, stupid." Carville was a strategist in Bill Clinton's successful 1992 U.S. presidential election against incumbent George H. W. Bush. His phrase was directed at the campaign's workers and intended as one of three messages for them to focus on. The others were "Change vs. more of the same" and "Don't forget health care."

9

Clinton's campaign advantageously used the then-prevailing recession in the United States as one of the campaign's means to successfully unseat George H. W. Bush.

In March 1991, days after the ground war in Kuwait, 90% of polled Americans approved of President Bush's job performance. During the following year, Americans' opinions turned sharply; 64% of polled Americans disapproved of Bush's job performance in August 1992.[1]

So in the middle of 2023, we find ourselves facing another presidential election cycle. It already looks like we are in for another carnival sideshow all the way up to election day, Tuesday, November 5, 2024. I have been thinking a lot about what is to come. What will the outcome be? Will it be a fair election? Will the voters believe it was? What will America look like one year after the next inauguration day?

The mainstream media keeps telling us that each side is so entrenched in their political ideology, that only a very small percentage of the voting population will make the difference. If entrenched Democrats make up 49 percent of voters, and the Republicans make up 49 percent of the voters, that leaves 2 percent to make the decision. The viewers are quick to accept their propaganda, not only what they say, but the unspoken premise of their shadowy agenda. If 98 percent of the people believe that only 2

---

1 Jennifer Agiesta, "Approval Highs and Lows," Behind the Numbers, Politics, The Washington Post, July 24, 2007, https://web.archive. org/web/20081012041134/http://blog.washingtonpost.com/behind-the-numbers/2007/07/approval_highs_and_lows.html.

percent of the people will make the difference, then why vote if I am in that 98 percent? Here is why! EVERY VOTE COUNTS! You do not get 49 percent of the vote, or 98 percent of the vote, **unless you vote**!

Most of the candidates have already formed their platforms and chosen their political teams to compete for the votes of the American citizenry. Some strategies have been formed while others are yet to be formed. And as of the fall, the season of primary debates is upon us.

Strategy is considered to be generalship or the art of managing armed forces in a campaign. It is sometimes called the science or art of maneuvering fighting forces in the presence of the enemy. While the candidate's purpose and philosophy should rarely change, the strategic plans must be constantly reviewed and updated when the markets and/or market conditions change. As we watch the field of those desiring to occupy the oval office, we wonder what should they do? And what will they do? What will we learn as the strategies reveal their true agendas? Who knows!

Was it not the statement of the plain, simple, fictional character, Forrest Gump, who rekindled a new generation of understanding when he said, "Stupid is as stupid does," meaning that man should be judged by his actions, not how he looks?

And then there is the quote, "We are all born ignorant, but one must work hard to remain stupid." Some have ascribed this statement to Benjamin Franklin, which may or may not be the case. It does, however, make a sobering point!

Unfortunately, much of the nation turns away from the political process thinking, "I've already seen this movie, and I know the ending!" Perhaps! But maybe, just maybe, there is a different ending. There might even be a new strategy!

So in the spirit and sarcasm of James Carville (as I do believe the economy plays a significant role in the voter's mind) and to respect the honest humor of Forrest Gump and to honor the wisdom of Benjamin Franklin, I declare unto you, the reader of this book:

"It's the CITIES, stupid!"

What do you mean? The CITIES? What about the CITIES?

No doubt, you have heard people say that the definition of insanity is "doing the same thing over and over and expecting a different result." Well, what are we doing differently? And what different outcome are we expecting to get? Is it time to take a second look? To challenge our own positions? Open our hearts and minds? I think so. Sure, the economy is important, but are there other important issues we need to address? Would it be to our advantage to address them? I think so!

Let me challenge you politicians out there, stop and ask yourself some simple questions. How did we get to where we are today as a nation? What was "right" in and for America for the last two and a half centuries? We are bombarded by the anti-America crowd with what is wrong with America from their perspective. What made it right? What was it that "worked" for us in a good way? What did not? Ask yourself this, "Am I an eternal optimist and not facing the realities of today? Or am I a 'negative Nellie' offering criticism without solutions, despair without hope?

Am I seeking personal gain at the expense of the crises of others? Or do I see their plight and quickly come alongside to help?" And we could keep on going with the questions, but the point I want to make to our leaders, and to the voting public, is this, "**Personal inquiry, coupled with brutal honesty, is the way forward**!"

SO WHAT'S IN A CITY?

In case you need a refresher course, there are concentrations of people in the cities of our nation. They are people just like you and me in many ways. They want a good life for themselves and for their children.

You will find the major cities have portions of the community that are made up of ethnic groups set apart and bound together by common ties of language, nationality, or culture. You know Chinatown, right? Which one? Oh, Manhattan? San Francisco? Or some other city? Many towns also have a Little Italy. Then there is DC's little Ethiopia or LA's Koreatown, San Jose's Little Saigon, and the list could go on and on. If you want their vote, you will need to meet them on their turf!

While holding on to ethnic identities is not wrong, it does carry with it the power to prevent and destroy a healthy future. Think about it for a moment. Consider the name "Asian American" or the "African American." I could call myself an "Irish American." These labels say, "keep looking back!" In so doing, one diminishes the power and resolve to look forward. Many chose to physically move away from the geographical past in order to pursue the opportunity of an American future. However, once here, the charlatans and race-baiters see an opportunity to drag the freedom seekers back home. In case you are having trouble seeing the problem, it is this—divide and conquer. Identify the groups and then plant improvised explosive devices and trigger them at just the right moment. You can learn from your past and appreciate your traditions, but if that is where you want to live today, then leave! Go back there! I prefer to stay here and look ahead at the opportunity, and the what ifs! As I do so, my dreams have not been shattered, and neither have they become nightmares. Tell the charlatan race-baiters to take a hike! They deserve neither power nor respect!

For many reasons, you find a concentration of low-information voters in these cities. It may be because of the poor education in most large cities. (Highly likely!) Perhaps it is the struggle for survival that occupies all their attention. It is hard to study and learn when you are hungry, starving, or working all hours of the day to pay rent or keep the lights on! Maybe it is the lack of access to information. It could be that the charlatans and media have become skilled at controlling them with propaganda. It would not be the first time in history that this was the case.

And then there is large! Large cities have large factories with large workforces who are members of large unions. There are large school districts and large demands on goods and services. Then there are the issues of crime and unemployment. When it happens in the city, it happens on a large scale. Do you want to do the math again! Large! Large! Large! How do you reach the "large"? You had better find a way!

Next to every urban area is a "suburban" area! They

are part of the major metro area. Do you know who lives in these suburban areas? Suburban moms. They have been a significant voter bloc for many election cycles. The pollsters are all quick to mention them. What is it about suburban moms? You don't know? Really! Well, you better find out, and you better build a strategy to reach them. Each one has a vote!

America's Largest Metro Areas[2]

1	New York-Newark-Jersey City, NY-NJ-PA	19,261,570
2	Los Angeles-Long Beach-Anaheim, CA	13,211,027
3	Chicago-Naperville-Elgin, IL-IN-WI	9,478,801
4	Dallas-Fort Worth-Arlington, TX	7,451,858
5	Houston-The Woodlands-Sugar Land, TX	6,979,613
6	Washington-Arlington-Alexandria, DC-VA-MD-WV	6,250,309
7	Miami-Fort Lauderdale-Pompano Beach, FL	6,129,858
8	Philadelphia-Camden-Wilmington, PA-NJ-DE-MD	6,092,403
9	Atlanta-Sandy Springs-Alpharetta, GA	5,947,008
10	Phoenix-Mesa-Chandler, AZ	4,860,338

---

2 Matt Rosenberg, "Most Populous Metropolitan Areas in the United States," Geography, ThoughtCo., updated April 7, 2022, https://www.thoughtco.com/largest-metropolitan-areas-1435135.

CHAPTER 1
MY FELLOW CITIZENS
AND CITY DWELLERS

It would be a good thing to remember what brought us together as a people. In just a few years, our nation may celebrate its 250th birthday. If not that, then we may all be grieving as the dirt is piled on America's casket of history past. Here is a brief overview of our beginning:

> Officially, the Continental Congress declared its freedom from Great Britain on July 2, 1776, when it voted to approve a resolution submitted by delegate Richard Henry Lee of Virginia, declaring "That these United Colonies are, and of right ought to be, free and independent States, that they are absolved from all allegiance to the British Crown, and that all political connection between them and the State of Great Britain is, and ought to be, totally dissolved."

> After voting on independence on July 2, the Continental Congress then needed to draft a document explaining the move to the public.

The Declaration has the words, "IN CONGRESS, July 4, 1776," at its top, because that is the day the approved version was signed in Philadelphia.

On July 8, 1776, Colonel John Nixon of Philadelphia read a printed Declaration of Independence to the public for the first time on what is now called Independence Square.[1]

DECLARED TO BE FREE—ACKNOWLEDGING THE TRUE KING

I am often challenged by the thought of what it must have been like for those brave souls who would stand up and make the declaration that they would no longer submit to the leadership of the king of England. Look closely at the Declaration and understand that their courage and resolve was a product of their faith in Almighty God, the Creator, the God of the Bible.

The Declaration of Independence

July 4, 1776—When in the Course of human events it becomes necessary for one people to dissolve the political bands which have connected them with another and to assume among the powers of the earth, the separate and equal station to which the Laws of Nature and of Nature's

---

1 Scott Bomboy, "When Is the Real Independence Day: July 2 or July 4?" Blog Post, National Constitution Center, July 2, 2023, https://constitutioncenter.org/blog/when-is-the-real-independence-day-july-2-or-july-4#:~:text=Officially%2C%20the%20Continental%20Congress%20declared,they%20are%20absolved%20from%20all.

God entitle them, a decent respect to the opinions of mankind requires that they should declare the causes which impel them to the separation.

We hold these truths to be self-evident, that all men are created equal, that they are endowed by their Creator with certain unalienable Rights, that among these are Life, Liberty, and the pursuit of Happiness. That to secure these rights, Governments are instituted among Men, deriving their just powers from the consent of the governed, That whenever any Form of Government becomes destructive of these ends, it is the Right of the People to alter or to abolish it, and to institute new Government, laying its foundation on such principles and organizing its powers in such form, as to them shall seem most likely to effect their Safety and Happiness.

Following this first portion of the Declaration of Independence, the founders laid out their grievances against the king of England. And then they ended their declaration with this courageously bold final paragraph:

We, therefore, the Representatives of the united States of America, in General Congress, Assembled, appealing to the Supreme Judge of the world for the rectitude of our intentions, do, in the Name, and by Authority of the good People of these Colonies, solemnly publish and declare, That these United Colonies are, and of Right ought to be Free and Independent States, that they are Absolved from all Allegiance to the British

Crown, and that all political connection between them and the State of Great Britain, is and ought to be totally dissolved; and that as Free and Independent States, they have full Power to levy War, conclude Peace, contract Alliances, establish Commerce, and to do all other Acts and Things which Independent States may of right do. And for the support of this Declaration, with a firm reliance on the protection of divine Providence, we mutually pledge to each other our Lives, our Fortunes, and our sacred Honor.

The premise of freedom and liberty is that every person has the right and opportunity to choose their life pursuits and enjoy the benefits resulting from those pursuits. Inherent in this freedom is personal responsibility, and as such, the individual may enjoy or endure the consequence of the choices they freely make. "All men are created equal" does not mean all people are alike, and it does not mean they all have the same things. It means they all have an equal opportunity to exercise their God-given rights. We call this "self-governing."

The "unalienable rights" are the rights that can never be forfeited, given away, or taken away. They are fundamental parts of humanity and the basis for moral interactions between people (the governed) and are irrevocable. These rights are bestowed upon us by God, our true King, not the king of an earthly nation!

A NATION IS BORN—
LAWS AND STRUCTURE DESIGNED TO SUCCEED

Once independence had been declared, our nation was formed with the writing of the Constitution that was ratified by the free people of the land. Ratification meant *to sign or give formal consent to (a treaty, contract, or agreement), making it officially valid.* Ratification was accomplished as the state legislatures, which had been elected by the people of each state, voted to adopt or reject the proposed constitution. A "yes" vote by 9 of the 13 states was required for ratification. The Constitution of the United States was finally ratified by all 13 states, Rhode Island being the last to sign on May 29, 1790.

The Preamble to the United States Constitution was written to explain the purpose of the Constitution. This is the establishment of human government in America. It reads:

> We the People of the United States, in Order to form a more perfect Union [United States], establish Justice [not equality], insure domestic Tranquility [peacefulness], provide for the common defence [make available for use; supply], promote the general Welfare [to further the progress of something, especially a cause, venture, or aim; support or actively encourage], and secure the Blessings of Liberty to ourselves and our Posterity [we can't create them, God is the one who grants the blessings of liberty], do ordain and establish this Constitution for the United States of America. [emphasis added]

21

The Constitution establishes our three branches of government who, in addition to having specific responsibilities, make up a series of checks and balances designed to keep the government from becoming corrupt, unlike the leadership of kingdoms, dictatorships, or tribal rulers who lack this level of accountability. The three branches are:

- **Legislative**—Established in Article 1 and includes Section 2, which establishes the House of Representatives. The representatives are elected from every state based on the proportion of the population of the state compared to that of the country, and they serve a two-year term. Section 3 establishes the Senate of which every state elects two senators. They serve a six-year term. The House of Representatives and Senate together make up the Congress. The powers of this Congress are enumerated in Section 8, limited in Section 9, and some powers are prohibited in Section 10. The primary responsibilities of Congress include the establishment of the laws and oversight of the executive branch. The power each congressperson has is in the form of a single vote.

  Article 1, Section 2 states, "The House of Representatives shall chuse [*sic*] their Speaker and other Officers; and shall have the sole Power of Impeachment."

  Article 1, Section 3 states, "The Senate shall have the sole Power to try all Impeachments. When sitting for that Purpose, they shall be on Oath or Affirmation. When the President of the United States is tried, the Chief Justice shall preside: And no Person shall be convicted without the Concurrence of two thirds of the Members present. Judgment in Cases of Impeachment shall not extend further than to removal from Office, and disqualification to hold and enjoy any Office of honor, Trust or Profit under the United States: but the Party convicted shall nevertheless be liable and subject to Indictment, Trial, Judgment and Punishment, according to Law."

- **Executive**—The executive branch is established in Article 2. The president is the leader of the executive branch and serves as the Commander in Chief of the Army and Navy and Militias of some states. The president is elected through the Electoral College to serve a four-year term. The Electoral College system ensures that one state does not dominate or determine who the president is. Every state participates and is important in determining the leadership of the nation. While some states, because of their size, have many votes, even a small state with few votes can become, in any election, the deciding votes.

  From his very title, we understand the president's responsibility is to execute the laws of the land as outlined in the Constitution. The Congress makes the laws, the president executes, or implements, the laws. The president is not intended or authorized to make the law!

  The president is required to take an oath which is set forth in the Constitution, Article 2, Section 1. The article states, "Before he enters on the Execution of his Office, he shall take the following Oath or Affirmation:—'I do solemnly swear (or affirm) that I will faithfully execute the Office of President of the United States, and will to the best of my Ability, preserve, protect and defend the Constitution of the United States.'"

The constitution is central in determining and directing the actions of the elected ones.

- **Judicial**—This branch is established in Article 3. There is one Supreme Court established, with the justices being recommended by the president and confirmed by the Senate. There are to be other inferior courts as the Congress may ordain and establish. These include federal courts, appellate courts, and circuit courts. The judges appointed to these courts sit in judgment of all disputes of the laws of the land. They are a check and balance on the other branches of the government. Their power arises from the Constitution, and they judge the process of a trial in order to bring a jury of peers to a verdict.

  The judicial branch does not make law, they do not implement or execute the law, they only judge the law. The courts are to follow the Constitution, not be persuaded by the culture! Think about this for a moment, if the courts were controlled by the ebbs and flows of the culture, what would our judicial system look like? Would it look like a little rudderless boat drifting randomly as the winds of change blew about? Would we have order, or would we have chaos?

CURRENT CONTROL—WHO IS IN CHARGE NOW?

In 2023, the progressive Democrats have control of the executive branch of the government. This includes the Department of Justice (DOJ), the FBI, the CIA, the IRS, and other agencies in that branch. This is a tremendous consolidation of power!

They also control the Senate as of fall 2023, which is one-half of the Congress, or legislative branch. The conservatives/Republicans now control the other half of the legislative branch, the House of Representatives.

The judicial branch is made up of various levels of courts. The Supreme Court has nine justices, six of whom were appointed by conservatives/Republicans and three by liberal/progressive Democrats. The lower courts have a mixture of appointees. Nominations to these courts are made by the sitting president and confirmed by the Senate. In 2023, one of the realities of the judicial branch is that conservative justices are primarily strict constitutionalists, meaning they base their decisions on the direct text of the Constitution and do not usually consider historical findings, and the liberal/progressive justices are not strict constitutionalists. Many are "activist judges" who interpret the law outside of the Constitution, often relying on historic happenings and judgments from other nations, in an attempt to create new laws through precedent. Judges are not supposed to be "lawmakers"!

Much of the skill set and strategy of the liberal/progressives today seems to me to be this—ignoring the Constitution of the United States, dodging the truth, and trying desperately to change the laws of the country by infiltrating the judicial system with activist judges. The judge's role is not supposed to be one of a law-maker. By being "activists," they themselves demonstrate a sense of lawlessness and the embracing of it. And they do this over and over which tells us they are intentional, not simply erring through ignorance. And the thing that is especially concerning to me is that it seems that in a party as large as the Democratic party, there would be some voices of these elected officials that would speak out against this kind of evil behavior, but those voices either do not exist, or they cannot be heard. And so, the lawlessness continues uninterrupted. What a dangerous pathway to tread!

SEEDS OF DESTRUCTION

The past few election cycles have demonstrated that the integrity of our election system has been compromised. A couple of examples from the presidential election in 2020 include the balloting in Milwaukee County, Wisconsin, where more votes were cast than there were registered voters. How does this happen? That is an obvious problem. Did some people vote twice? Did someone who was not eligible cast a vote? Did some poll worker, government official, or ballot counter manufacture multiple votes? Any of these scenarios indicate something being done illegally. It was a strategy, not an accident or flaw in the system!

Also, on election day evening, as votes were being tallied, some of the outcomes were reported as numbers that included fractions of numbers. For illustration purposes, one candidate having 103,206.**3** votes and another 87,500.**7** votes.[2] How could a candidate get a fraction of a vote? To me, that indicates that there was a computer programming issue. Each vote cast was reported as something other than a single, whole vote. No one votes by splitting their votes into "tenths" of a vote. This may have been an unintentional defect, or it could have been an intentional alteration. Whichever the case, it manifests as either multiplying the impact of a single vote or dividing a single vote by a certain percentage. For example, if one vote was actually cast, the computer was programmed to only count that vote as 8/10 of a single vote, which would mean that if there were 100 votes cast, only 80 would be reported as having been cast. Or if 100 votes were cast that were tallied at 1.3 votes per vote, those 100 votes would be reported as 130 votes. These examples demonstrate obvious corruption!

WHERE DID THE SEEDS GET PLANTED?

Any person who follows politics understands that the Left has strongholds on both coasts, and those strongholds are primarily in the major cities in our country. These cities would include Los Angeles, San Francisco, Seattle, and Portland on the West Coast, and cities such as Boston, New York, and Philadelphia on the East Coast. There are also strongholds in between, and once again, they are

---

2 For further study, Mara Nale-Joakim, "Claims of US Election Fraud: Fractional Voting," Medium, January 1, 2021, https://maranailejoakim. medium.com/claims-of-us-election-fraud-fractional-voting-b5cc13cbe936.

centered in major cities such as Chicago, Atlanta, Saint Louis, Detroit, Denver, and the list could go on.

The political right is stronger in the Midwest and South where a good percentage of the voting population is rural or from smaller communities. If you are interested and would like to take the time, just look back at the presidential election cycle in 2020 and ask yourself where the controversies occurred. This will likely show you where the seeds of corruption and destruction were planted.

Assuming that all the election problems will not be fixed for the election in 2024, the GOP needs a strategy to infiltrate these democratic strongholds and capture as many votes from them as they can. You don't have to be a rocket scientist to see that the general voting bloc for Democrats are controlled by corrupt politicians and leaders, and that the general voting public are kept ignorant or are being intentionally deceived. The latter is possible because a very high percentage of the mainstream media is in bed with the liberal progressives.

So the question for the GOP becomes, "How can you reach them?" The media is corrupt, the educational systems are corrupt, most social media companies are corrupt and are illegally censoring conservatives and Republicans. Twitter, now known as "X," exposed that! The public service and teachers' unions are corrupt and providing extraordinary financial support to the progressive Left (even conservative Republican money is aiding the Left! That should not be!). Is there any possible way to penetrate these political megaliths? The Hollywood elites and the major professional sports leagues also seemed to be driven by liberal progressives in their pursuit of big money. These are difficult odds to overcome. It is not a job for rookies, novices, and inexperienced fighters to do alone! America needs a proven champion to lead the comeback!

So one can see that the seeds of the destruction of America have been sown, and they have been germinating and growing for decades. Before long, the full fruit of this evil orchard will be on the tables of every American citizen (and the tables of all illegal aliens too). What is a God-fearing patriot to do? Retreat to their political bunker? Flee to a remote island in the Arctic Ocean and just hang on? We'll find out in chapter six!

CHAPTER 2

THE END WILL COME SUDDENLY

Is it too late now that we have recognized our error? There will be an end to all this evil and corruption you know, and it will likely come suddenly. When it comes, where an individual stands will likely influence their experience for the rest of their life on planet earth, and perhaps, for all of eternity. Please bear with me in this next chapter to lay some theological groundwork that is eerily parallel to what we are experiencing in our world today.

SOMEONE SEES YOU NOW!

You remember the opening to "Santa Claus Is Comin' to Town"? It is likely that most of us have heard this song many times during our lifetime. Does it make you wonder why it was written? Was it just to celebrate a season, or introduce us to a source for toys? Was this song a parent's ploy to get their kids to behave? That does seem plausible as it is talking about future behavior for which one should watch out for. So you should not cry, and you better not pout, and here's why: somebody's coming in the future, and it will influence whether or not he treats you well or poorly! Cute song but certainly a cruel fear tactic if you really drill down to discover its real purpose!

Well, it is true that someone is watching. It's not Santa Claus, though. It is Almighty God! And whether a person believes in God or not, God's eyes are beholding the good and the evil that person does. His Word says so! And so, there is no real argument about who is right.

The phrase "the eyes of the Lord" is found several times in the Bible, and it carries the idea that God sees everything and will hold those who he sees accountable for what they do. You might say there is a righteous judgment coming. It seems as though judgment and accountability are closely aligned to this phrase. The following are some instances where we find the phrase in the Bible:

"But Noah found grace in the <u>eyes of the</u> Lord" (Genesis 6:8; emphasis mine). In this case, God spared Noah and his family from the judgment of the world-wide flood. Only eight people out of the entire population of the world at that time were delivered from the wrath of God. God knew everything about all of them and chose to save only eight! I would encourage you to read 2 Peter 2:1–22 and see how a just and merciful God handles those who follow the messages of the false prophets. That will make you wonder!

Moses wrote to the people, "A land which the Lord thy God careth for: the <u>eyes of the</u> Lord <u>thy God</u> are always upon it, from the beginning of the year even unto the end of the year" (Deuteronomy 11:12; emphasis mine). This was a promise to the nation of Israel that God cared for them and was always observing the actions and circumstances of their nation.

Moses also said, "When thou shalt hearken to the voice of the LORD thy God, to keep all his commandments which I command thee this day, to do that which is right in the eyes of the Lord thy God" (Deuteronomy 13:18). God, as their Creator, determined what was right for mankind, and he required obedience to his commandments to ensure it happened, and he was watching to see if the people obeyed. That is accountability.

King David's family would be blessed for generations that followed him because David sought to obey God all the time. It was the desire of his heart, not perfect obedience, which brought about this blessing. God forgave David's sin and blessed his obedience: "Because David did that which was right in the eyes of the Lord, and turned not aside from any thing that he commanded him all the days of his life, save only in the matter of Uriah the Hittite" (1 Kings 15:5).

The first thing recorded in the historical book of 2 Chronicles 14 about the boy king named Asa, King David's great-great-grandson, is: "And Asa did that which was good and right in the eyes of the LORD his God." He is only 11 or 12 years old when this is said of him. He is ascending to the throne of his nation, Judah, which was part of the divided kingdom of Israel. God saw the behavior of this adolescent boy and commended him for it, memorializing it for all of history.

Later in King Asa's reign, he would make an error in judgment and demonstrate a weakness in his faith. It may be that his successes had made him overconfident and less dependent on God. That does come through in the story. God would send a prophet along with this reminder: "For the eyes of the LORD run to and fro throughout the whole earth, to shew himself strong in the behalf of them whose heart is perfect [upright] toward him. Herein thou hast done foolishly: therefore from henceforth thou shalt have wars" (2 Chronicles 16:9). Asa's response to the messenger was not good, and Asa became a bitter man, oppressed his people, and soon became sick and died. God witnessed everything in Asa's life! What a lesson for us to learn because he is watching each of us too. And to me, that is the lesson. Not just Asa's behavior, but how God is watching the affairs of mankind. And in this case, God was seeking to find something so he could act further. What would God do with us if ours was the upright heart he found? I wonder!

David included this statement in a tremendous song of praise for God's working in his life: "The eyes of the LORD are upon the righteous, and his ears are open unto their cry" (Psalm 34:15). He had sought the Lord's help and received it in an overwhelming way. Now, through this Psalm, he encourages the people to trust God and cry out to him in their time of need. He sees, he hears, and he will answer!

David's son, King Solomon, learned this same great truth from his father. In Solomon's desire to instruct his son, he repeats this wonderful concept in his book of Proverbs. "For the ways of man are before the eyes of the LORD, and he pondereth all his goings" (Proverbs 5:21). God ponders the ways of man, meaning that as God observes the ways of man, he makes man's way smooth. This is an incredible thought. We often focus on what God helps us do. How often do you think about what he has kept you from doing? That is the idea here.

He also said, "The eyes of the LORD are in every place, beholding the evil and the good" (Proverbs 15:3). Nothing escapes the ever-watching eye of the all-knowing God. Nothing!

In Proverbs 22:12, Solomon said, "The eyes of the LORD preserve knowledge, and he overthroweth the words of the transgressor." The Lord always guards the truth, especially the truth of the Bible. He overturns or subverts the deceitful words of those who oppose the truth. I cannot begin to count the number of times I have told my kids, "Don't worry, the truth always wins!" It does! Always!

And there are many other places in Scripture we find the eyes of God observing man. I will end this line of thinking with a quote from the Apostle Peter: "For the eyes of the Lord are over the righteous, and his ears are open unto their prayers: but the face of the Lord is against them that do evil" (1 Peter 3:12). This is an encouragement to the righteous and a warning to the sinner in the age in which we are currently living. God sees us, hears our prayers, and opposes those who do evil. If we have chosen to be on God's side, he is on our side! If that has not been our choice, then by default, we become the enemies of God, and he is against us! Go ahead! Try to contend with him. You have already lost when you rejected him—judgment and accountability! Is God your Savior or judge?

GOD'S WORD HAS NEVER FAILED. YOU BETTER LISTEN TO WHAT HE HAS TO SAY!

One of my favorite Psalms is Psalm 119. It is the longest Psalm in the Bible, and it is a Psalm in the Word of God about the Word of God. And one of my favorite verses is verse 89, "For ever, O LORD, thy word is settled in heaven." This is such a key to life. As one invests their time and energy to read, study, and meditate on God's Word to learn about their role and responsibility, and then begin to apply it to their own life context, they can do so with the assurance that halfway through the game of life, the truth will not change. God's Word is settled. And God does not and will not change his thinking or his mind about that. He said, "For I am the LORD, I change not" (Malachi 3:6). It matters not what part of the world you may live in, or what your economic status might be, or what your family or culture has historically believed or taught you, God's Word will not change. Someone once said, "What you believe does not change the truth." True! Since we cannot change the truth, and we cannot be successful in contending with God, then the appropriate thing to do would be to let the God's truth change us!

Jesus made some incredible statements about the Word of God. He said, "For verily I say unto you, Till heaven and earth pass, one jot or one tittle shall in no wise pass from the law, till all be fulfilled" (Matthew 5:18). Jots and tittles are basically accent marks mean-ing the smallest of things. "And it is easier for heaven and earth to pass, than one tittle of the law to fail" (Luke

16:17). Nothing that God has stated in Scripture will go undone! Absolutely nothing! It is not God's Word that will fail, it is men who will fail to heed God's Word.

WHEN TRUTH FALLS IN THE STREETS

Isaiah the prophet is prophesying against the Jewish people in chapter 59 of the book of Isaiah. Their sins are great and many. Isaiah was reminding them that if they would repent of their sinful ways and turn back to God, he was ready to hear them and save them. Their sin had separated them from fellowship with God and had cost them his power in their lives to do right. The behavior Isaiah describes is unimaginable, and even more so to think this characterized the behavior of God's chosen people. Sin was getting worse and worse, and increasingly frequent, to the point that it seemed like justice and judgment had no impact, and the people were trampling on the truths of God's Word as if they were the cobblestones in an old city street. Isaiah describes it like this: "And judgment is turned away backward, and justice standeth afar off: for truth is fallen in the street, and equity cannot enter" (Isaiah 59:14). The people had no respect for God, for God's Word, or for the servants of God. They felt invincible and impervious toward God. There was no discernment and no justice found in the people. Black lives didn't matter, brown lives didn't matter, yellow lives didn't matter, red lives didn't matter, and white lives didn't matter either! Nobody mattered! Chaos reigned! God did not fail, the people failed.

Every time I read this chapter it is like Isaiah is describing modern-day America. We are truly living in an era when truth, or good, is called evil, and evil is called good. What must God be thinking today? We know he is watching!

The case against the truth is being built day by day, and judgment is coming! The greatest author of all time is writing the biography of every person, and for those who have been rejected, those biographies will be used in their final court proceedings! "And I saw the dead, small and great [the big sinners and the little sinners], stand before God; and the books were opened: and another book was opened, which is the book of life: and the dead were judged out of those things which were written in the books, according to their works" (Revelation 20:12).

SPEAK UP MAN OF GOD

In the face of a powerful king and nation of England, those who signed the Declaration of Independence showed tremendous courage and strong resolve with their actions even without an organized defense to rely on. Many of the signers were Bible believers, perhaps 52 of the 55 signers had a personal relationship with God.[1] They stood on the truth and relied on the power and providence of Almighty God.

I wonder if they were encouraged by the same passage from which we should draw encouragement and strength for the times in which we live:

---

1 The Oakland Press, "Declaration Signers Were Christians," News, The Oakland Press, last updated June 17, 2021, https://www.theoaklandpress.com/2004/03/27/declaration-signers-were-christians/.

Finally, my brethren, be strong in the Lord, and in the power of his might. Put on the whole armour of God, that ye may be able to stand against the wiles of the devil. For we wrestle not against flesh and blood, but against principalities, against powers, against the rulers of the darkness of this world, against spiritual wickedness in high places. Wherefore take unto you the whole armour of God, that ye may be able to withstand in the evil day, and having done all, to stand. Ephesians 6:10–13

Paul exhorts these soldiers of Christ to put on the equipment God has issued to them and be prepared to engage the enemy. He and his minions are on the attack! Get ready to "stand in that evil day"!

It is time to stand up and to speak up! Just saying that brings to my memory one of the saddest situations in history that is recorded in the Scriptures. God sent the prophet Ezekiel to warn the people of Jerusalem and the entirety of God's people. Here is the event:

And the word of the LORD came unto me, saying, Son of man, say unto her, Thou art the land that is not cleansed, nor rained upon in the day of indignation. There is a conspiracy of her prophets in the midst thereof, like a roaring lion ravening the prey; they have devoured souls; they have taken the treasure and precious things; they have made her many widows in the midst thereof. Her priests have violated my law, and have profaned mine holy things: they have put no difference between the holy and profane, neither have they shewed difference between the unclean and the clean, and have hid their eyes from my sabbaths, and I am profaned among them. Her princes in the midst thereof are like wolves ravening the prey, to shed blood, and to destroy souls, to get dishonest gain. And her prophets have daubed them with untempered morter, seeing vanity, and divining lies unto them, saying, Thus saith the Lord GOD, when the LORD hath not spoken. The people of the land have used oppression, and exercised robbery, and have vexed the poor and needy: yea, they have oppressed the stranger wrongfully. And I sought for a man among them, that should make up the hedge, and stand in the gap before me for the land, that I should not destroy it: **but I found none**. Therefore have I poured out mine indignation upon them; I have consumed them with the fire of my wrath: their own way have I recompensed upon their heads, saith the Lord GOD. Ezekiel 22:23–31 [emphasis mine]

An evil conspiracy had consumed and corrupted the culture. It resulted in the decline of leadership, and this was at the heart of their problem. Notice who was leading the conspiracy—the prophets. These religious leaders should have been representing God to the people and delivering God's messages. That was the divine role of the prophets of God. They represented God to the people. Instead, they were destroying the culture and the faith of the people and the people themselves, destroying lives and homes.

They did their evil work by daubing them "with untempered morter." That would be analogous to building a brick structure with bad cement. What was built to endure for generations would be destroyed in short order. These messengers of God were altering the messages that God wanted delivered and lying to the people about what God really said. Their messages were not messages of deliverance—they were messages of deceit and destruction. This was a dereliction of duty of the highest order.

Next in line in the conspiracy were more religious leaders—the priests. In contrast to the role of the prophet, the priest's responsibility was to represent the people before God. They were the ones who would receive the sacrifices from the people, prepare them, and then present the sacrifices of the people to God, making atonement for the people. They were critical in restoring and reconciling sinful men to a holy God. Instead, they had violated the laws of God, compromised the holiness of God (which, by the way, would be akin to condoning the sinful behavior of the people and smearing God's reputation), and profaned the name of God in the public square, effectively making God of no significance or relevance in the minds of the people. Their hypocrisy ruled the day. Faith was in great decline, and the faith of many was destroyed forever.

The ungodliness of the religious leaders, with no appearance of consequence, emboldened the political class. So third in the conspiracy were the princes—the civic and political leaders of the nation. They were supposed to provide the protective governance of the people that would allow the people to live quiet and peaceable lives. Instead, the fruit of their work was chaos and corruption. Fear, not peace, became the experience of the common man, and it was for the princes' own personal financial gain. Their profiteering was at the expense of the people.

With these leaders corrupted, the prophets, the priests, and the princes, the people were soon discouraged, and then, seeing no way forward, they turned on each other. Selfishness rose to the top of each one's priority list. Evil began to dominate the culture. Morality was in steep decline. The "survival of the fittest" was now the law of the land. Oppression of the poor and robbery were the weapons of this warfare. It vexed or frustrated the people into hopelessness and homelessness. AND GOD SAW ALL OF IT HAPPENING! AND HE KNEW THE HEART OF EVERY PARTICIPANT!

So what would he do? Send another worldwide flood? Rain down fire and brimstone from heaven to destroy the wicked? Would he exact vengeance on the world? **What did God do?** He sought for a man! It was the merciful God of heaven, the very one the people ignored, rejected, and offended who initiated a rescue plan. And in an incredible show of mercy and grace, he looked for a man. Just "a" man. One man! One who would choose to be God's man.

Where did God look for a man? He looked "among them." He was looking for someone—a man, a surrendered, willing man, who might be found in the midst of this chaotic and corrupt people! As his eyes scanned the multitudes, back and forth, to and fro, profession by profession, he was looking for a man.

What would God do with the man? What could one man do? God would have the man "stand" before him in the gap of his protecting hedge, filling the space that sinful men had made as they trampled on the righteousness of God. He would use the man to stand, stopping the sinful decline of a wayward people while God himself went to work repairing the vineyard he had planted generations earlier. Remember what God's messenger had said to King Asa? "For the eyes of the LORD run to and fro throughout the whole earth, to shew himself strong in the behalf of them whose heart is perfect [upright] toward him" (2 Chronicles 16:9). One willing soul would stave off the destruction of the judgment of God, and it was possible with the power of God working in one man. He just wanted the man to "stand"!

GOD WAS LOOKING AND LOOKING AND LOOKING! Who? When? Where?

And then we read some of the saddest words recorded in the Bible, "***But I found NONE!***" Not one single soul in the nation would stand up! How awful! How sad! How shameful! The sinful hearts of selfish men rejected the loving, compassionate, appeal of the merciful, loving God of the universe. No one amongst his chosen people would answer his call.

Rejection is a powerful force! For mankind, it is painful to endure and difficult to overcome. For God, perhaps painful, but it would not stop him. Difficulty was no barrier—it was an opportunity to show himself powerful!

So what happened? True to his Word, God poured out his indignation and consumed them with the fire of his wrath, executing justice and judgment. Soon, the nation would not be scattered to the four corners of the world where they would live in exile for the next two and a half millennia, equivalent to 2,500 years!

NEVER BEFORE AND NEVER AGAIN

Never before in the history of America have we witnessed the anti-God corruption we are seeing today. The evil actions of the leadership of our nation now include four recent indictments, carrying nearly a hundred charges, against a man who sacrificed the freedom, comfort, and privacy of his family and a successful business career, to serve as the 45th president of the United States. And, by the way, who donated the compensation for his service to his country right back into the government.[2]

Although executing his duties and delivering on his promises better than any president in our lifetime and having to endure two sham impeachments and guiding a nation and world through the devastating effects of a man-made, worldwide epidemic, he was wildly successful in ending wars, fixing a teetering economy, rebuilding a gutted military, providing tax relief to the nation, and much more.[3] Now, even as the former president of the

---

2 Adam Andrzejewski, "President Donald Trump Probably Donated His Entire $1.6M Salary Back to the U.S. Government – Here Are the Details," Policy, Business, Forbes, February 27, 2021, https://www.forbes.com/sites/adamandrzejewski/2021/02/27/president-donald-trump-prob-ably-donated-his-entire-16m-salary-back-to-the-us-government--here-are-the-details/?sh=1296e9761a8d.

3 Trump White House, "Trump Administration Accomplishments," uploaded January 2021, accessed October 21, 2023, https://trumpwhitehouse.archives.gov/trump-administration-accomplishments/.

United States, he remains under the immense pressure of political persecution and is the current front-running political opponent of one who may be the most corrupt president in the history of the United States. This is unprecedented in the history of our country. Evil, through its socialist and communistic puppets, is doing all it can to maintain its grip on a hurting people.

The legal actions against Donald Trump appear to be creatively novel and grossly unconstitutional. However, if these enemies of the state are successful in convicting Donald Trump by holding court proceedings run by activist judges in jurisdictions where Democrats and Progressives have a hate bias against Trump, a sham trial like this may be the last time it happens in the history of the United States. The rule of law would be so compromised, and our government so corrupted, that this nation will cease to be the nation that our founders intended and that God has blessed in the past. America as we know it would be no more! The storm clouds of finality are gathering, my friend!

WARS AND RUMORS OF WARS, BUT THE END IS NOT YET!

Matthew 24 records the conversation between Jesus and his disciples about some of the future events in the world that then was. In verse 3, the disciples come to Jesus privately and say, "Tell us, when shall these things be? and what shall be the sign of thy coming, and of the end of the world?" They made this request because Jesus had just spoken to a multitude of Jewish people describing the corruption that was in their day and the horrible effect that it would have on the people. The disciples had begun to understand that the religious crowd, including the leadership, had turned their back on God, and judgment was about to come. God's truth was marching on!

The Jewish nation had so rejected the Messiah, the one whose coming had long since been prophesied in their religious teachings, that it would not be long now before Jesus would close the door of opportunity for them to be reconciled to God. Once that door was closed, God would open the door of opportunity for reconciliation and redemption to the Gentile nations.

That opportunity for the Gentiles would be known as, "the times of the Gentiles" (Luke 21:24) or as we refer to it—"the church age." Christ would use his apostles to take the good news of the gospel to the world. Those who believed the gospel and repented of their sin would be saved from the judgment of God. The redeemed believers would form the body of Christ, also known as the church. This time of the Gentiles would continue for 2,000 years or more. We are living in this age right now!

The Scriptures record Jesus' answer:

> And Jesus answered and said unto them, "Take heed that no man deceive you. For many shall come in my name, saying, I am Christ; and shall deceive many. And ye shall hear of wars and rumours of wars: see that ye be not troubled: for all these things must come to pass, but the end is not yet. For nation shall rise against nation, and kingdom against kingdom: and there shall be famines, and pestilences, and earthquakes, in divers places. All these are the beginning of sorrows.

Then shall they deliver you up to be afflicted, and shall kill you: and ye shall be hated of all nations for my name's sake. And then shall many be offended, and shall betray one another, and shall hate one another. And many false prophets shall rise, and shall deceive many. And because iniquity shall abound, the love of many shall wax cold. But he that shall endure unto the end, the same shall be saved. And this gospel of the kingdom shall be preached in all the world for a witness unto all nations; and then shall the end come. Matthew 24:4–14

Now, stop and think with me for a moment. Could this possibly be a description of the times in which we are currently living? Does this sound familiar to you? How much like this description was Ezekiel's prophecy against Israel? My friend, the storm clouds of history are forming once again! Daniel's prophecy of the history of Israel, commonly referred to as the 70 weeks of Daniel, would tell of 490 years of God dealing with Israel as a nation. Israel's exile lasted approximately 2,500 years. The "church age" or the "times of the Gentiles" in which we live has gone on for nearly 2,000 years now. Just as the disciples who asked Jesus, we too wonder, "How long, O Lord?"

THE TRUMPET WILL SOUND

There will be a sudden end to the age we just described. The Apostle Paul describes this to the Thessalonian church. In Paul's first letter to the Thessalonians (who, by the way, were relatively new believers, young in the Lord), he writes:

> But I would not have you to be ignorant, brethren, concerning them which are asleep, that ye sorrow not, even as others which have no hope. For if we believe that Jesus died and rose again, even so them also which sleep in Jesus will God bring with him. For this we say unto you by the word of the Lord, that we which are alive and remain unto the coming of the Lord shall not prevent [precede] them which are asleep. For the Lord himself shall descend from heaven with a shout, with the voice of the archangel, and with the trump of God: and the dead in Christ shall rise first: Then we which are alive and remain shall be caught up together with them in the clouds, to meet the Lord in the air: and so shall we ever be with the Lord. Wherefore comfort one another with these words. 1 Thessalonians 4:13–18

Paul also teaches us of this event as we read of it in our Bibles, an event many theologians refer to as "the next major event on God's calendar of prophecy." They mean that there is nothing more that needs to be fulfilled on God's prophetic timeline before you and I hear a trumpet blast come suddenly from heaven. All the believers from the church age will be caught up together in an instant to meet Jesus Christ in the clouds, and they will forever be with him. The description of this event was to be a comfort to the believers of Paul's day, and if you are truly a born-again, blood-bought child of God, these should be comforting words to you too.

This event would also begin a new dispensation, the tribulation. This would be the final seven years of God's prophesied dealings with the nation of Israel. And in case you missed the relevance, Israel, after being scattered for more than 2,500 years, was reformed as a nation in 1948, the same year this author was born. The Jews have returned into the land, just as the Lord had promised Abraham approximately 4,000 ago. The 2,500-year exile is over, it ended in my lifetime, and the clock of judgment is ticking!

SUDDEN DESTRUCTION WITHOUT REMEDY

After Paul left Thessalonica, having started the church there, some false prophets came in amongst the people and were teaching these new believers that they were already living during the tribulation. That prospect frightened the people of the city, especially the new believers. And so, Paul wrote a second letter addressing this in order to comfort the people. Starting in chapter 2, Paul said,

> Now we beseech you, brethren, by the coming of our Lord Jesus Christ, and by our gathering together unto him, That you be not soon shaken in mind, or be troubled, neither by spirit, nor by word, nor by letter as from us, as that the day of Christ is at hand. Let no man deceive you by any means: for that day shall not come, except there come a falling away first, and that man of sin be revealed, the son of perdition; who opposeth and exalteth himself above all that is called God, or that is worshipped; so that he as God sitteth in the temple of God, shewing himself that he is God.

Remember ye not, that, when I was yet with you, I told you these things? And now ye know what withholdeth that he might be revealed in his time. For the mystery of iniquity doth already work: only he who now letteth will let, until he be taken out of the way. And then shall that Wicked be revealed, whom the Lord shall consume with the spirit of his mouth, and shall destroy with the brightness of his coming: Even him, whose coming is after the working of Satan with all power and signs and lying wonders, And with all deceivableness of unrighteousness in them that perish; because they received not the love of the truth, that they might be saved. <u>And for this cause God shall send them strong delusion, that they should believe a lie: That they all might be damned who believed not the truth, but had pleasure in unrighteousness</u>. 2 Thessalonians 2:1–12 [emphasis mine]

This passage helps us understand what it is to have the door of opportunity closed by God. Paul was telling the Thessalonians, those who were saved and part of the church, they did not have to worry about this happening to them. They were securely saved in Christ and could as Paul put it, "rest with us." It was the unbelievers who had shunned God's offer of the free gift of eternal life that would now face eternal judgment. No rest for them.

Perhaps Solomon gives us the mind of God better than anyone when he taught his son this principle: "He, that being often reproved hardeneth his neck, shall suddenly be destroyed, and that without remedy" (Proverbs 29:1). Sudden judgment! No remedy!

HERE COMES THE JUDGE!

"You can deny God, but you cannot escape him!" I heard this quote many years ago. As trite as some may think it to be, it is absolutely true! No one will miss their court date with God!

Because the people that had heard the gospel before that trumpet sounded and had rejected it, God closes the door of opportunity to be saved. At that moment they are "damned." In other words, their final judgment is determined and declared.

It is a dangerous thing to snub your nose at the mercy and grace of God. Here is how the writer of the letter of Hebrews describes the consequence of the foolish choice:

> For if we sin wilfully after that we have received the knowledge of the truth, there remaineth no more sacrifice for sins, But a certain fearful looking for of judgment and fiery indignation, which shall devour the adversaries. He that despised Moses' law died without mercy under two or three witnesses: Of how much sorer punishment, suppose ye, shall he be thought worthy, who hath trodden under foot the Son of God, and hath counted the blood of the covenant, wherewith he was sanctified, an unholy thing, and hath done despite unto the Spirit of grace? For we know him that hath said, Vengeance belongeth unto me, I will recompense, saith the Lord. And again, The Lord shall judge his people. It is a fearful thing to fall into the hands of the living God. Hebrews 10:26–31

HELL, THE LAKE OF FIRE, AND ETERNAL TORMENT

King Solomon speaks of the finality of those who die without a redeemer. He wrote, "When a wicked man dieth, his expectation shall perish: and the hope of unjust men perisheth" (Proverbs 11:7). Take a moment and give this verse a second look and some serious thought. It is telling us that at the time of the physical death of a person who has not been reconciled to God ALL HOPE IS LOST! FOREVER!

Luke 16 gives the account of a rich man who is dead without being reconciled to God and is currently being tormented in hell and contrasts that with the death of a beggar who is secure in the arms of God. This passage reveals some of the torments and hopelessness of hell.

Revelation 19 and 20 tell us of the lake of fire and the final judgment of the unsaved of all the ages. Although we looked at this earlier in this book, let's be reminded of what the Apostle John wrote, describing this judgment in Revelation 20. He says,

> And I saw a great white throne, and him that sat on it, from whose face the earth and heaven fled away; and there was found no place for them. And I saw the dead, small and great, stand before God; and the books were opened: and another book was opened, which is the book of life: and the dead were judged out of those things which were written in the books, according to their works. And the sea gave up the dead which were in it; and death and hell delivered up the dead which were in them: and they were judged every man according to their

works. And death and hell were cast into the lake of fire. This is the second death. And whosoever was not found written in the book of life was cast into the lake of fire. Revelation 20:11–15

This is the description of the final judgment for unbelievers of all the ages. Their everlasting dwelling place is determined, and it is a place where they will suffer the tormenting fires of the undiluted wrath of God forever, no rest day or night (Revelation 14:11)! No one in their right mind would risk the chance of this destiny! It is the lake of fire.

You see, there is a penalty for sin, for evil! It is death, or separation, from God (Romans 6:23). Every sin or evil act any person ever commits is observed by the all-seeing eyes of the Lord and recorded in books in heaven. And unless God forgives that person's sins, they will personally pay their sin penalty.

I have heard many people express doubt about a literal, fiery judgment, or they believe that the stories of Luke 16 and Revelation 19 and 20 are allegorical or analogies. I imagine they do so to ease the thoughts of guilt and the possibility of facing such a judgement. Luke 16 seems to be a story of some real people. The rich man was identified as a "certain" rich man, and the beggar was identified as Lazarus. In no other parable did Jesus use a proper name. In this account, not only does he mention Lazarus, but Jesus also mentions Abraham, the father of the Jewish nation. It was the hope and desire of every Jew when they died that they would go to be with Father Abraham.

And then, regarding the lake of fire, Matthew 13 offers some incredible insight. Early in the chapter Jesus is asked a pointed question and immediately he gives a clear response. Here is the incident:

> And the disciples came, and said unto him, Why speakest thou unto them in parables? He answered and said unto them, <u>Because it is given unto you to know the mysteries of the kingdom of heaven, but to them it is not given</u>. . . . And in them is fulfilled the prophecy of Esaias, which saith, By hearing ye shall hear, and shall not understand; and seeing ye shall see, and shall not perceive: For this people's heart is waxed gross, and their ears are dull of hearing, and their eyes they have closed; lest at any time they should see with their eyes and hear with their ears, and should understand with their heart, and should be converted, and I should heal them. Matthew 13:10–11, 14–15 [emphasis mine]

By telling an earthly story using figurative language, he makes it clear that he was revealing literal truth with a heavenly meaning to some in his audience, while concealing it from others.

In this chapter, he gives the parable of the sower, the parable of the tares among the wheat, parable of the mustard seed, and the parable of the leaven. After the parable of the leaven, the disciples gathered to him privately and asked what the parable of the tares meant. In Jesus' response to their question, he rehearses the figurative words of the parable and gives the literal translation in his explanation, which I will put in bold in the following text. Jesus Christ is clearly teaching there will be a fiery judgment for all unredeemed sinners. With that in mind, look at his explanation:

He answered and said unto them, <u>He that soweth</u> the good seed **is the Son of man**; <u>The field</u> **is the world**; the <u>good seed </u>**are the children of the kingdom**; but <u>the tares</u> **are the children of the wicked one**; The <u>enemy that sowed them</u> **is the devil**; <u>the harvest</u> **is the end of the world**; and <u>the reapers</u> **are the angels**. As <u>therefore the tares are gathered and burned in the fire</u>; so shall it be in the end of this world. **The Son of man shall send forth his angels, and they shall gather out of his kingdom all things that offend, and them which do iniquity; And shall cast them into a furnace of fire: there shall be wailing and gnashing of teeth.** Then shall the righteous shine forth as the sun in the kingdom of their Father. Who hath ears to hear, let him hear. Matthew 13:37–43 [emphasis mine]

This is when reality becomes real! This is why the gospel of Jesus Christ is so important. It is the only way a sinner can avoid this judgment. Have you accepted the person of Jesus Christ as your Savior? If not, right now is the time to receive him. Stop right now, and in sincere sorrow in your heart and mind for your sin, and with a genuine desire to be saved from its penalty, by faith, ask Jesus to save you. The promise from his Word is this, "For whosoever shall call upon the name of the Lord shall be saved" (Romans 10:13).

CHAPTER 3

WHO IS YOUR LEADER, AND WHERE ARE THEY TAKING YOU?

A LEADER MUST HAVE FOLLOWERS, OR THEY ARE NOT A LEADER

This may be an obvious statement, but it needs to be said: one may think they are a leader, feel like they are a leader, or believe they are a leader, but if they have no followers, they are not a leader!

That being said, put your thinking cap on for a moment! From where or from whom, does a leader get their power? In reality, it is from the followers they have, although the leader would be reluctant to admit that. Ego, you know! Every person has a choice to be a follower or not. If they choose to follow, they empower the leader. If they choose not to follow, there is no power given. "Take me to your followers!"

So, to me, that makes the following question extremely important: "Why would I want to follow that person?"

At the heart of our problems in America today is the lack of thought one gives to the question before they become a follower of another. Some give no thought and blindly follow someone "just because." They never get to the "why?" Others give little thought. This is often driven by laziness or a lack of interest or concern. They make little or no investment of time and energy to determine the "why." Their default position is, "This is what I have always done."

The clever politicians and false teachers of our day understand this and see these people as "easy prey"! I have often heard these people referred to as "low-information voters." Promise them a cell phone, and you get their vote. Or give them a pack of cigarettes in exchange for letting you help them fill out their absentee ballot, and they kindly accept your offer to deliver it for them to the ballot drop box. Who got the person's vote was not as important to the low-information voter as the pack of cigarettes or the cell phone was. And these fools would soon reap a harvest of misery that they never intended as they sowed the seed with a careless or carefree vote.

WITH NO ACCOUNTABILITY THEY BECOME A REPEAT CUSTOMER

Because little attention is paid by these easy targets and with two to four years between elections, the politicians see them as low-hanging fruit. The politician spares little expense or effort in reaching them, knowing that facts and information are of minor importance to the voter and that party loyalty is of greater importance to them. These voters are enticed through emotion to become repeat customers, buying into the deceitful and dishonest promises and platforms of corruption because they are angry, offended, victimized, sad, or whatever other emotions can be stirred up by the deceitful Hollywood TV ads that are skewed and shadowed to bolster their effect. The ads do not even have to be truthful to be believed and embraced by this crowd. The emotional appeal is enough to win the day, and so, they vote.

Although the theme of our economic system is characterized by this phrase, "let the buyer beware," the phrase is rarely referenced in the political marketplace. The intent of the phrase is that buyers take responsibility for the condition of items they purchase and should examine them before purchasing them. If they do not, oh well! They must live with the consequences of their lazy choice, with no recourse or redress. The marketplace of the votes is no different.

WHAT HAVE YOU DONE FOR ME LATELY?

Before you give your allegiance to someone you might ask yourself, "What have they done for me lately?" And what may be more important than giving your allegiance is casting your vote. When you vote for something, you are also voting against something. And it would do you well to take time to understand what it is you are voting for and what it is you are voting against and how that influences your life. You know, "just the facts, ma'am," or "the truth, the WHOLE truth, and nothing but the truth."

Here are a couple current examples about some

controversial issues. Would you consider voting for open borders because you are compassionate toward those coming from abroad who are seeking a better life? Would you vote for open borders if you thought it meant killing 100,000 of your friends and neighbors each year because it made it possible for evil drug lords to traffic fentanyl? How compassionate would that be to your friends and neighbors?

And would you vote to allow abortions up until the time of giving birth, to appease the desire of a woman who accidently conceived in a moment of passion, even though her health was in no danger because you wanted to protect her rights to do with her own body as she pleased? Would that be the same as condoning sinful behavior? If you are so concerned about the rights of others, then what would your thoughts and feelings be toward the rights of the unborn child who had no say in the decision? Why would you approve of killing them? Would it be morally right to kill a baby that God had given life to in the womb of a mother? Would it be okay with you to try to explain your vote endorsing this practice to God? In person?

We should be interested in following leaders who knew what was right and would do what is right! Those who would have courage and honesty to stand up for what God stands for. Why would you choose to follow a God rejector? What would you expect to gain? Would you be putting yourself in eternal jeopardy? How would you be able to pillow your head at night?

HOW IS THAT WORKING OUT FOR YOU?

Sometimes, we as voters are so focused on one or two issues that we give little attention to the other things an elected politician does. If we are not careful and diligent, in exchange for favor on one issue, we accept the evil and ungodliness of the rest of the work or platform of the politician. We end up voting for something we did not want!

Politicians are notorious for promising one thing and then, after being elected, doing another or even doing the opposite thing. This is an integrity issue. Is that not what the "shell game" is? If you really want a good read on the person's integrity, look at all the areas of their life, including their family, their work, their service, their faith, and so on! Who are their friends? Then listen carefully to what others are saying about them.

It is quite common nowadays for members of a political party to claim to stand up for an ethnic community, community of color, or country of origin. An honest appraisal of the recent past in our political history in America clearly reveals this strategy. You know, "If you don't vote for me, then you ain't black." That statement was horribly offensive to many people, but it revealed the racist heart of the one who said it, Joe Biden.[1] The party or politician makes promises to the community but never delivers. Then, four years later, they show up with the same promises, the same bag of tricks, and seduce the community into voting for

1 Astead W. Herndon and Katie Glueck, "Biden Apologizes for Saying Black Voters 'Ain't Black' if They're Considering Trump," *The New York Times*, last updated January 20, 2021, https://www.nytimes.com/2020/05/22/us/politics/joe-biden-black-breakfast-club.html.

them again. I characterize their dirty little tactics as political prostitution. It is that shameful! The cycle perpetuates generation after generation with little or no benefit to the voter. "Once a party member, always a party member." If that is your mantra, you are the repeat customer! Get on the ship! Take a seat! Sit down! Shut up! I'm taking you to your leader!

It would do any person good to look back at previous election cycles and consider the people they voted for. What was it they promised that they would do when they were put into political office? Did they fulfill their promises? Or did they fail to fulfill them? Make yourself a list. Put the politician to the test. If they did fulfill their promises, what was the influence on your life? Are you happy with the outcome? How is that working out for you?

WHAT WOULD THE LOSS OF FREEDOM REALLY MEAN TO YOU?

I know that the political news may not be of great interest to many, but it is in the arena of politics where the battle for your freedom is lost or secured. Who you vote for, and the policies they hold, has a direct influence on your freedom and freedoms.

The Constitution says the certain inalienable rights of our life, our liberty, and our pursuit of happiness are at the core of the purpose of our nation. What would the loss of these freedoms really mean to you in everyday life? What would they mean to your kids? What would life be like if you lost them? How would your community operate if there were jackbooted thugs policing your every move?

Are there examples in history from which we can learn about people who have lost their freedom? Yes! Do the terms "ethnic cleansing" and "holocaust" come to your mind? How about "mass graves"?

I have seen firsthand what it would mean. I spent two extended trips into the former Soviet Union in the early 1990s. The people were living in constant fear of the tyrannical government. Their housing was small, cramped, and without many conveniences. In a home, the wife spent as many hours a week waiting to get bread, which provided barely enough food for the family, as her husband spent working in a government-owned factory. There was little or no medicine and health care to meet basic needs. Alcoholism was rampant in the country. And the military presence was intimidating. The elite communist leadership was prospering greatly while the general public suffered, living in poverty. I saw with my own eyes the extraordinary wealth displayed by the elite at The Armoury in the Kremlin and the opulence of the restored Winter Palace of Catherine the Great. And then I could contrast it with the poverty and despair of the people we ministered to, sat with, spoke to, or shared a crust of bread with. Those clever leaders who cried out for equality had no intention of living it! It was an emotional appeal to deceive the people and gather followers. Before long, the followers became subjects—and many of them prisoners.

If there was any liberty in the Soviet Union/Russia, it was only a "perception" of freedom. The KGB, much like our FBI and CIA, monitored everyone. As long as the people toed the communist line, they perceived themselves to have liberty. To them, liberty was simply the lack of conflict and oppression at the moment. Never was it viewed as an opportunity for expression or prosperity. The pursuit of happiness—in other words, the decision to do whatever you wanted to pursue to make your life enjoyable by your standards—did not exist. People even quit dreaming about it as a possibility.

There is an evil conspiracy of leadership in our nation that is driving our country in the same direction and toward the same fate. They will continue to do so as long as they have followers, as ignorant and unconcerned as they might be. I just cannot imagine any resident of America desiring to live like the common folks of a communist-led country. They would not choose it if they knew what it was genuinely like. "Let the buyer beware!"

Just recently, I heard for the first time in mainstream media the use of the term "un-American progressive Left" used to describe the Democratic party. It was not used by a biased, Republican politician, rather, a pundit of their own party used it! Was it a slip of the tongue? Or did he mistakenly identify their true agenda, making America un-American?

As a resident of a large city, have you ever considered how much freedom you really have or could have? It seems like our understanding of freedom is often blurred by the barriers created by our concrete jungles. The vehicle congestion and smog keep us at home or indoors where we avoid seeing the real issues. The massive crowds of people can intimidate us or frighten us into seclusion. The webs of interstates and limited access highways that blanket our cities are boundaries that fence us in. The media moguls conspire to keep much of the true news from our eyes and ears in order to keep us penned up.

Information suppression was a primary tactic of the communist leadership. If the people did not know what they did not know, then the government could easily control the people. Once again, with my own eyes, I saw the rooftop devices that scrambled the radio and TV signals of Radio Free Europe. Please, please allow me to suggest this warning to every American: if you are locked into one or two channels of media, i.e., CNN, NBC, CBS, ABC, FOX, and the like, diversify your intake of information. Don't allow them to seduce you with a favorite TV anchor or podcast host. Their organizations are driven by intentionally communicating a narrative they want you to believe.

Have you ever stood on a mountaintop and breathed the cool, fresh air? Have you experienced the aromas of the Midwest fall as the soybean and corn harvests were taking place? Have you ever gone fishing on a body of water so large you did not see another boat or fisherman all day? Have you walked barefoot on a sandy beach beside the roaring ocean? You won't find these experiences in the city! Can you imagine driving through miles and miles of orchards in the Central Valley of California, relishing in the blossoms of the nut trees in the spring or bathing in the aroma of the ripening pears or peaches in the summertime? Can you even imagine the sense of peace and serenity or the mystic smells of the giant redwood groves in the forests of Northern California? Have you witnessed the breathtaking views of the Grand Canyon or felt the mist and roars of Niagara Falls? Have you seen the boiling pots, geysers, buffalo herds, and other unusual sights in Yellowstone, or have you seen the deserts of Southern California as they come alive after the smallest of rain showers? If you haven't experienced these, your appreciation of the freedoms you possess has some growing to do.

Today, you have the freedom to experience any or all of these wonders. But that freedom could be gone overnight! What would you do? What could you do? Who are you following, and what are they up to? Where are they taking you? Why are you following them? You had better find out! It is your own freedom that is at stake! And you better exercise the limited power you do have—VOTE!

YOU CANNOT SEE THEIR HEART, BUT BY THEIR FRUIT, YOU SHALL KNOW THEM

The Bible teaches us that we cannot know the heart of another individual or see into a person's mind to know for sure what they are thinking. We cannot know their true feelings even though we can observe the outward effects of some of those feelings. The Bible does teach us "by the fruit ye shall know them." By observing what someone does, we can know them. What they DO, not what they SAY, will tell us what they actually believe. The only problem with accepting that approach is this, you do not find out what they really believe until they have done what they actually do. Wow, is that not a mind bender?

It is foolish to blindly follow someone or take them at their word without having first observed their integrity. You know the old saying, "Fool me once, shame on you. Fool me twice, shame on me!" Former president Ronald Reagan was famous for his approach to addressing this conundrum by employing the following principle, "Trust, but verify!" This is great advice! Don't just settle for what they say, follow up to see what they did.

If you want to put yourself to the test to see how you have been doing in this area, use this little exercise to evaluate yourself. First, think about the person you voted for in the last election. Have you got their name in your mind? Now, what promises did they make that appealed to you? You may want to write them down: it will help your thinking process.

Once your list is complete, then, beside each promise, write out a brief narrative of how you think they actually did in fulfilling that promise. Do not use feelings! Do a little research and get some facts that would support your narrative. Inspect the fruit! Then, compare your narrative to the promise. How did they do? Was it different than what they said they would do. (WARNING: do not stay "ticked" off too long for being a sucker and getting fooled!)

IGNORANT OR INTENTIONAL

Now take your little test to the next level. There is no doubt that as we observe some of what goes on in our culture that it makes you shake your head in wonder. How could somebody be doing that? Or why would they be that way? Why would somebody want America to have an open border and allow evil people to propagate their influence through drug peddling and human trafficking? Why would that be acceptable behavior to me? Are they just ignorant about the consequences or outcomes of their actions? Or are they intentional and trying to create chaos and bring about destruction?

Quite often, evil people use deceit or diversionary tactics to avoid revealing to others their true agenda. It is a strategy often employed by politicians, false teachers/prophets, and community activists. You have undoubtedly heard the phrases "sleight of hand" or "the shell game." These describe tactics used to conceal agendas because the one using them knows that if people knew what the real agenda was, or what they were really up to, they would never follow them.

You have to now exercise some discernment, which requires serious thought. We are now trying to examine motives! We see the fruit, but why was this the fruit that was produced? Did the farmers not know what they were doing when they planted the trees or vines? Were they ignorant about what kind of fruit would be the result of their farming? Or were they intentional? More than likely, in fact a very high percentage of the time, the farmers were intentional, knowing what the fruit of their labors would be.

And so it is with the politicians, intention more than ignorance is driving them. And they are intending to prey upon the ignorant, low-information crowd to advance their agenda. Have you ever considered that all they see in you is IGNORANCE? Care for you and benefit to you is not even on their radar! It does not make their "Top 10 List of Reasons" they are running for their office and why they are pursuing you. In fact, care for you and benefit to you is not anywhere on their "list of reasons." The only place it appears is in their sinister strategy plan to garner votes.

FALSE PROPHETS MAKE MERCHANDISE OF YOU

The Apostle Peter, in his second letter to the true believers from the dispersed nation of Israel, warns his audience that there would be false prophets among the people then even as there would be false teachers among us in our day. He says that they would privately or cunningly bring in damnable heresies or harmful teachings. They would have shadowy, sinister agendas. They would even deny the Lord who had died for them, meaning they rejected God's offer of forgiveness and gift of eternal life. That kind of behavior, in God's eyes, would bring upon themselves swift destruction, and deservedly so.

The sad thing to me about the false teachers is what Peter says in 2 Peter 2:2, "many shall follow their pernicious [evil] ways." In other words, these false prophets would seduce them to follow their leadership, and in so doing, these evil prophets would accomplish their sinister agenda. One of the strategies the false prophets would use was to "speak evil of the truth."

That's an interesting statement because it provides a way for us today to identify a false prophet. If these clever teachers are instructing people in things that are contrary to the Bible, then the Bible exposes them as a false prophet. So, in a sense, you can use the Bible to inspect the fruit, and in fact, you should use it. In case you missed it, this exposes the true battlefield of life—the battle for truth takes place in our minds. You can already read about the battle. You will find it in the Bible, all the way from Genesis 3 where we find its beginning to the very end of Revelation 20 where it culminates! It is a remarkably interesting read! If you haven't read it yet, I highly recommend it!

And then Peter talks about the false prophet's methods and their motives. Their motive of covetousness makes them use hypocritical words to "make merchandise" of the people. Here is the real agenda, personal financial gain! Do we see this happening in our day? If not, it is because you have not bothered to look or do any research about those you are following. If you have been suckered into following one or more of these clever charlatans, you may want to ask yourself if you have any ostriches in your family tree? Especially those who were attracted to sandy holes in the ground. (If you do, you may want to encourage them to avoid beaches!)

My observation of politicians in our time has been this: "Some people get rich and go to Washington, while other people go to Washington and get rich." It is not a difficult exercise to research and find out that those that are serving in elected offices have gathered extraordinary wealth while serving on a congressman's or senator's salary for decades. Just look at the last two presidents, (clue: 45 and 46). Be honest about what you find. Is there a contrast? Do not let a bias cloud your judgment!

Have you ever asked yourself why personal enrichment of politicians, especially career politicians, happens or how this happens? Are you aware that Washington and the politicians there do not "generate" revenue or "create" wealth? It is the taxpayers of America that generate revenue and send it to Washington. Once the money is in the government's coffers, the politicians make laws and maneuver money to their advantage. They use the power of their office and that wealth to make laws and influence others who are willing to share their wealth with the politician. While this is not legal in most cases, it is the reality of politics. The bottom line is that you and I are being used to advance their godless agendas, and all the while, they are building their personal wealth. In the meantime, we keep struggling to meet day-to-day needs for ourselves and our family.

ANTI-GOD POLICIES

One way you can discover much about the heart and motive of a politician is to examine the policies that they put forward. An honest look at politics in America would reveal there is corruption in both major political parties. It would serve you well to ask yourself which party's platform and policies best line up with the truth found in God's Word. (WARNING, yes, another WARNING, learning this may be harmful to your understanding; however, you will find it helpful if your desire is in line with God's desire for your life). And so (ANOTHER WARNING: your bias may be exposed and challenged, proceed no further if you choose to remain ignorant, i.e., willingly ignorant), here are some of the policy issues: (don't you hate the interruptions and captions that they use to distract people from knowing the truth? Okay. You can proceed!)

Policy—Abortion on demand: Abortion is an intentional decision to kill a baby. God is the giver of life to that baby. (Was this issue renamed in the Woke Dictionary because someone did not like the word "murder"?)

Policy—Open borders: This policy allows for a

flood of crime and creates a huge financial burden on the taxpayers of America. The lawless benefit while the law-abiding are damaged. Boy! Is this not an issue as disconcerting as the approaching bank of thick fog on a cool San Francisco morning? Where is the line between compassion and criminal behavior? Do not ask this question of a Californian politician, they don't know either. And don't ask your representative, they are afraid to give you an answer until they know your personal position. You can expect their answer to be in the form of another question too. Frustrating, isn't it? And don't forget, protests intimidate them too.

Hey! Why are they giving me the finger? Oh, that finger! They are just checking to see what direction the winds of opinion are blowing.

Policy—The promotion of spending and expansion of debt: This practice destroys a healthy economy. Last year, our national debt exceeded the thirty-trillion-dollar mark. In case you need figures to help you understand, that looks like this: $30,000,000,000,000.00. Contrast that to your hourly rate of $15.00. Wow! Eleven more zeroes!

There is a lot of money spent in Washington to give political favors or to pay back someone who has helped a politician accomplish a secret agenda. Senator Rand Paul publishes annually his "Festivus Report of Government Waste" where he highlights the spending of the government. (WARNING: get a bucket, towel, and wet washcloth before reading. You will likely need them all. Oh yeah, and the smell will be highly intolerable.)

This year, I am highlighting a whopping $482,276,543,907 of waste, including a steroid-induced hamster fight club, a study to see if kids love their pets, and a study of the romantic patterns of parrots. No matter how much money's already been wasted, politicians keep demanding even more.[2]

Why would you tolerate this foolishness with your tax dollars? Wait! Bad question! Who DO you tolerate? "Stupid is as stupid does!"

Policy—Abandonment of the Constitution: There has long been a philosophical debate between the conservative and the liberal/progressives as it relates to constitutional interpretation. The debate is between "originalism" and "living constitutionalism." In an article written in 2019 titled "Originalism Versus Living Constitutionalism: The Conceptual Structure of the Great Debate," Lawrence B. Solum, the author, frames the issue this way: "Originalists argue that the meaning of the constitutional text is fixed and that it should bind constitutional actors. Living constitutionalists contend that constitutional law can and should evolve in response to changing circumstances and values."[3] In order to execute their "flexible

---

2 Rand Paul, "The Festivus Report 2022," Rand Paul US Senator Kentucky, released December 23, 2022, https://www.paul.senate.gov/wp-content/uploads/2023/02/Festivus-23-clean-12.22-v2.pdf.

3 Lawrence B. Solum, "Originalism Versus Living Constitutionalism: The Conceptual Structure of the Great Debate," Scholarship, UVA Law, 2019, https://www.law.virginia.edu/scholarship/publication/lawrence-b-solum/953451#:~:text=Originalists%20argue%20that%20the%20meaning,to%20changing%20circumstances%20and%20values.

laws theory," liberal/progressives appoint activist judges to the bench at every level possible. And as technical as this may seem, there is another obvious abandonment of the Constitution—namely, simply refusing to enforce existing written law. Or they try to enforce laws that you cannot read because they are not written! Anyone supporting this foolishness is supporting lawlessness. You might think, who cares? So now, let me get you really ticked off!

It seems to me that the Democrat party has often acted in opposition to the Constitution since the party began. They were on the wrong side of the civil rights laws by promoting segregation. They have been on the wrong side of the life issues, especially in the areas of abortion and euthanasia. They are constantly challenging constitutional rights that were so important in the formation of our country. They attack the First Amendment right to freedom of speech by collaborating to sensor the public on social media. They constantly assault the Second Amendment right to bear arms, including trying to legislate possession out of the hands of the law abiding—all the while, understanding that the nature of the criminal is to break the law. What is the real motive behind such an action? And, how about the success of "gun-free zones"? Have you notice that these zones seem to be the places where most mass-shootings take place? Chicago, Illinois, is considered to have some of the strictest gun-control laws, yet week after week, the news headlines reveal the statistics of the policy failure. In the five-year period from 2019 to 2023, police department statistics identify 3,138 murders, an average of more than 12 per week.[4] There, are you mad at me or mad at them? It makes me think of the words of the Apostle Paul after rebuking the sinful practices of a church that was being led astray. He asked, "Am I therefore become your enemy, because I tell you the truth" (Galatians 4:16).

Can you imagine how the value of a community's real estate would drop if you had to advertise that the house you had for sale was in "a community without laws or law enforcement, and where you can no longer have weapons to defend yourself?" Who in their right mind would want that? You see, the Constitution does matter to you—especially if you live in New York, Baltimore, Philadelphia, Cleveland, Detroit, Chicago, San Francisco, Seattle, Portland, Phoenix, or Los Angeles! Say "hi" to your mayor and city council for us!

Policy—The destruction of the family: The first institution God created was the family, Genesis 2 in the Bible. Anyone choosing policies that destroy or damage the family is anti-God! That is just a fact! Consider the following inconvenient truths:

> Among children who were part of the "post-war generation," 87.7% grew up with two biological parents who were married to each other. Today only 68.1% will spend their entire childhood in an intact family.[5]

> With the increasing number of premarital births and a continuing high divorce rate, the proportion of

4 Brandon Johnson and Larry Snelling, "CompStat: Report Covering the Week of 20-Nov-23 Through 26-Nov-23," Chicago Police Department, accessed December 5, 2023, https://home.chicagopolice.org/wp-content/uploads/1_PDF-sam_CompStat-Public-2023-Week-48-1.pdf.

5 Fathers.com, "The Extent of Fatherlessness," accessed November 11, 2023, https://fathers.com/the-extent-of-fatherlessness/.

children living with just one parent rose from 9.1% in 1960 to 20.7% in 2012. Currently, 55.1% of all black children, 31.1% of all Hispanic children, and 20.7% of all white children are living in single-parent homes.[6]

White children born in the 1950–1954 period spent only 8% of their childhood with just one parent; black children spent 22%. Of those born in 1980, by one estimate, white children can be expected to spend 31% of their childhood years with one parent, and black children 59%.[7]

If these statistics don't bother you, try considering the heart and words of Jesus. He was having a teaching time with his disciples instructing them about relationships and their response to offenses that may threaten them: "Then said he [Jesus] unto the disciples, It is impossible but that offences will come: but woe unto him, through whom they come! It were better for him that a millstone were hanged about his neck, and he cast into the sea, than that he should offend one of these little ones" (Luke 17:1–2).

Did you catch it at the end? Jesus loves little children, all children. When someone abuses or mistreats a child or abandons them for selfish or fleshly pursuits, when the children experience the "offenses," in God's economy, the offender is worthy of death—death by millstone and a deep body of water.

The politicians and profiteers who are using the

6 Fathers.com, "The Extent of Fatherlessness."

7 Fathers.com, "The Extent of Fatherlessness."

destruction of the family to advance their evil agendas are in BIG TROUBLE WITH GOD! You might say to yourself, or even out loud, "I don't believe that!" What you believe does not change the truth. You better let the truth change you, or you too are in BIG TROUBLE WITH GOD!

Policy—The rejection of male and female as the only genders: God created only two genders, male and female. That's it! Two! Not three, not four, or some abstract, undefinable number or concept you might be wrestling with in the twisted mind of the culture.

> Genesis 1:26–27 says, "And God said, Let us make man in our image, after our likeness: and let them have dominion over the fish of the sea, and over the fowl of the air, and over the cattle, and over all the earth, and over every creeping thing that creepeth upon the earth. So God created man in his own image, in the image of God created he him; male and female created he them."

You do not get to determine your gender! God does! Your gender is intentional and no accident. It is part of God's plan for you. Each gender has a specific role that was determined by God. It is his design, and he has a purpose in it. (If you are thinking you don't like this, you can take the argument up with God. But in the end, he always wins!)

Procreation is one of those purposes—establishing families to procreate to keep the generations coming! God's primary command to Adam and Eve, the first couple, was "be fruitful and multiply."

As with everything God created, mankind was created with distinction. As male and female, they are intentionally unique and are born out of God's creative genius.

I came to understand through my study that some of God's creatures have intuition, others have instinct, but mankind is unique in that he has intelligence. Intuition is built-in understanding, without needing to logically reason. An example might be a sunflower. It intuitively turns its flower toward the sun, and it follows the sun throughout the day. The little sunflower does not have a mother that says, "Okay, 'sunny,' turn 10 more degrees toward the sun." It turns intuitively.

Some of God's creation has instinct—an innate, typically fixed pattern of behavior. Such as animals that respond to certain situations that happen, i.e., "bees have an instinct to create hives."

And finally, mankind was distinctively given intelligence, which is the ability to learn information and develop skills. Man also has intuition and instinct. For man, this is especially important as it places him into a unique relationship with Creator God, and it equips him to "exercise dominion" over the animal kingdom.

Thus, as a living soul, man can learn of and relate to God. This relationship is unique and vital to understanding the true purpose of life. And this relationship also unlocks the truth and significance of the teachings of the Bible, which I consider to be God's instruction manual for mankind. Please allow me to encourage you, do not be foolish like many of us men, use the instruction book!

Policy—Giving school boards authority over children instead of parents: God has given the parents responsibility and privilege of raising and training children. Consider the instruction God told Moses to give to the nation of Israel:

> Hear, O Israel: The LORD our God is one LORD: And thou shalt love the LORD thy God with all thine heart, and with all thy soul, and with all thy might. And these words, which I command thee this day, shall be in thine heart: And thou shalt teach them diligently unto thy children, and shalt talk of them when thou sittest in thine house, and when thou walkest by the way, and when thou liest down, and when thou risest up. And thou shalt bind them for a sign upon thine hand, and they shall be as frontlets between thine eyes. And thou shalt write them upon the posts of thy house, and on thy gates. Deuteronomy 6:4–9

And then, the Apostle Paul gave instruction to the church families at Ephesus about their roles and responsibilities:

> Children, obey your parents in the Lord: for this is right. Honour thy father and mother; which is the first commandment with promise; That it may be well with thee, and thou mayest live long on the earth. And, ye fathers, provoke not your children to wrath: but bring them up in the nurture and admonition of the Lord. Ephesians 6:1–4

The progressive Left appears to consider children their responsibility with authority greater than that of the parent. They are wrong! While "a village" may be helpful to the parent, the parent must raise the child. ("It Takes the Parents"—what a great T-shirt slogan.)

The primary purpose of the school is to "support the parents" as the parents raise their own children. The school should not "supplant the parents." It is public education's privilege and responsibility to help parents raise their children by providing academic instruction. The National School Boards Association (NSBA) and the teachers' unions will oppose this position every step of the way and at all costs. One might conclude their mantra to be "Don't Tread on Our Indoctrination Camps!"

Primary among the academic subjects are mathematics, reading, writing, history, and geography. These are foundational subjects one needs to engage and compete in the world. Everyone benefits when we know these subjects. And they are subjects that seem to have an influence on a daily basis in the average person's life.

Local school boards in recent decades have bowed to the power and pressure of the national teachers' unions to establish their policies, agendas, and budgets. The agenda of those unions should be restricted to negotiating issues of compensation and workplace conditions. It is not their responsibility to raise the children who belong to the parents of the community. The NSBA is not necessary and only drains local schools of much needed funding.

In recent years, school board meetings have become battlegrounds where board members and parents clash instead of being a place where support and cooperation lead to policies that benefit the kids. School boards have been driven to provide and promote political and moral agendas that break down the family unit and promote secularism in the culture in opposition to the truths of Almighty God. Their sinister agenda is to dumb down the students in order to reduce and eventually eliminate the middle class. This opens the door to what is considered a classless society characterized by communal living where the serfs do what they are told, or else! This really is Communism, but it is more tolerable if we call it "Socialism" (Hmmm, words? Those pesky words!). The dirty little secret is that there really are classes—the ruling elite and the "also-rans"!

Before you cast your vote, let me encourage you to consider the platform, or agenda, of the one you intend to vote for. Here is why. **Your vote for the person is a vote for the policy!** On judgment day, how will you explain your vote to God? You are accountable to God, not the politician! The personality won't matter then, it will be about the policies you supported.

THE EVIL TRIANGLE IN THE BLACK COMMUNITY

In a recent television interview, I watched a black minister speak about "the evil triangle in the black community." He declared that those in the triangle represent the "worst of the blacks, not the best." Then he defined the participants of the evil triangle. It was made up of black preacher/pastors, black civil rights leaders, and black politicians. This was not the first time I had heard the term. Quite a few years ago, I read an interesting book. I'll settle here for pointing you to it with the following:

> Since its inception the Democratic Party has been led by a group of immoral people consumed with

81

death and madness. Like rodents and fungus thrive in the darkness and filth of a sewer, they thrive in the darkness and filth of politics. When given the option they supported slavery over freedom, death over life, forced segregation over brotherhood, chaos over family, identity politics over merit, law-lessness over order and open borders over sover-eignty. They no longer recognize charm, grace and elegance but celebrate, the vile, the grotesque and the abnormal. It's a place where the Iron Triangle fits very well.[8]

As I listened to the interview, I could not help but think of the stereotype, often depicted in movies and tele-vision programs, of a black pastor. He would be wearing an expensive suit, flashy shoes, and classy hat as he was driving his tricked-out Cadillac through the poor neigh-borhoods of his congregation. Not only is this a TV ste-reotype, but it is also an "observable reality"!

Then, with my thinking cap on, I realized how often during tragic events in the black community that a "Rev-erend Al" or "Reverend Jesse" would show up with a camera crew in tow. As one Chicago politician is famous for saying, "never let a crisis go to waste!" The careful observer would quickly notice that these gainsayers would twist circumstance and fact to shape a narrative they could skillfully use to stir up the emotions of a hurting people. How ungodly is that?

---

8 Vince Everett Ellison, *The Iron Triangle: Inside the Liberal Democrat Plan to Use Race to Divide Christians and America in their Quest for Power and How We Can Defeat Them* (Outskirts Press, 2019).

Some have thought the real interest and expertise of these charlatans was that of "corporate shakedown." Under the guise of nonprofit, charitable work, these shakedown artists would accumulate enormous personal wealth. Have you ever asked yourself, "Are they really a pastor? or a civil rights champion? or a political activist?" Wow, a self-contained evil triangle! All three in one untidy package! How could this be? This does bear some resemblance to the evil triangle this minister was describing during the interview. We cannot judge their hearts, but you can see the fruit, and what they do!

Sometime ago, I authored an article I titled "**Gotcha Sucker**!" and posted it on my social media. I thought it might be appropriate and encouraging to include it in this book, so here it is:

No one likes to be fooled. Being the victim of a huckster or charlatan is a humiliating experience. It can provoke responses ranging from despair to revenge seeking.

Consider these familiar characterizations for a moment; someone referred to as "snake-oil salesmen" or "used-car salesman." The intended message of the characterization is that they make their living by deceiving those they pretend to serve. They offer one thing but deliver another; bait and switch so to speak. One could characterize them as *Sucker Seekers* because that is what they are doing: looking for the sucker who would take their bait. Most often they are proactive, not passive, in their mission of deceit as they look for their next opportunity or target.

Taking a stand for someone, or a position on

something, only to find out later that you were fooled is humiliating. It undermines confidence and trust. We become skeptical or cynical if it happens frequently. If we are not careful and discerning, our blind loyalty can lead to these unfortunate circumstances. Perhaps more often it is the result of our rash, emotional decisions, or reactions. The truth is that the damage is done by the time discovery is made! "*Gotcha Sucker*!"

Recently, I heard a man ask this question, "What would you do, or how would you react, if you just found out that everything you believed was based on a lie?" A loaded question for sure, but how would you answer it? King Solomon, in all his wisdom, warned his son to avoid embarrassing situations like these when he taught him this simple truth: "He that answereth a matter before he heareth it, it is folly and shame unto him" (Proverbs 18:13).

"Answering a matter" has the idea of responding to an issue that has entered your life experience. "Before he heareth it" means the response or reaction happened before you had all the facts or understood all facets of the issue. All of us can be quick to form opinions or take positions! No denying that! If, however, we respond prematurely, we tend to make a fool of ourselves or do something shameful. Solomon's message is quite simple. To form an opinion or determine an action before having all the facts leads to foolish, shameful reactions and outcomes.

So what if we don't have the facts? What is it that drives our "decision mechanism"? Why do we react or respond so prematurely? The answer to these questions may expose the strategy of the deceiver! Consider the following and see what you think.

Emotions are real, and they are a part of every person's soul. Emotions are not inherently bad. However, emotions, when they become the dominant ingredient in decision-making, become the lighted fuse that can lead to foolish or shameful explosions. They can contribute to bad outcomes.

The "rational soul" basically includes the intellect, the emotions, and the will and is often referred to as the "heart of man." The "intellect" is what you know; the "emotions" are what you feel. Both feed into your "will," the decision-making mechanism in your life. It is your God-given gift and right to make choices. The will is where we determine "I will" or "I will not" do something. It is our response or decision to the "matter" Solomon was talking about, or any matter for that matter.

The skilled deceiver presents himself or his case and will then attempt to brush past our intellect and appeal primarily to our emotions. They seek an "uninformed decision" from us to accomplish their agenda. They understand that they can successfully advance their mission by undermining our intellect simply by stirring our emotions. We become "low-information voters." Clever, but sinister! Oh, and by the way, emotional decisions are usually made very quickly.

So here is the point: whenever someone is seeking to have you follow, endorse, or approve them, get your intellect into high gear and control your emotional responses by saying to yourself, "Wait a minute" or "Let me check that out." Count to 10 or to 1,000 if necessary!

It is okay to take time before committing to a decision or answering a matter. A right answer is always better than a quick answer! Listen to what they say, but then put what they have said to the truth and knowledge test. Do not just act on what you hear, but consider what you can see as well before acting or reacting! What someone has done may be quite different than what they said they would do. Another wise teacher simply stated, "By their fruit ye shall know them" (Jesus Christ to his disciples, Matthew 7:20).

This simple truth has broad application in life. Whether it is in the marketplace where commerce happens, the religious world where doctrines are propagated, or the political world where votes are the prize, it is appropriate to get the facts and control our feelings before "answering a matter." It is vital to even our important relationships in life, whether it is husband and wife, parent and child, employee and employer, or friend and foe. To avoid shameful, destructive outcomes, do not be hasty. Take time to get the facts! The truth always wins!

Consider this: we are held accountable in every circumstance of life by what we do, not how we feel or even by what we believe. It is what we DO! So be intentional and anchor yourself to truth.

WHAT IN THE WORLD IS A BANANA REPUBLIC?

Is it a T-shirt? Is it a retail clothing store? A trendy bar or restaurant? I wonder what your immediate response was when the question was posed. Did geography or politics even cross your mind? According to ThoughtCo.,

> A banana republic is a politically unstable country with an economy dependent entirely on revenue from exporting a single product or resource, such as bananas or minerals. It is generally considered a derogatory term describing countries whose economies are controlled by foreign-owned companies or industries. . . . By exploiting the labors of the working class, the oligarchs of the ruling-class control the primary sector of the country's economy, such as agriculture or mining. As a result, "banana republic" has become a derogatory term used to describe a corrupt, self-serving dictatorship that solicits and takes bribes from foreign corporations for the right to exploit large-scale agricultural operations.[9]

Characteristics of a Banana Republic

The way the phrase *banana republic* is used has evolved since it was introduced more than a century ago. "It is no longer limited to countries in Central America or the tropics. Key characteristics of a banana republic in the modern world include":[10]

---

9 Robert Longley, "What Is a Banana Republic? Definition and Examples," History & Culture, Humanities, ThoughtCo., last updated November 19, 2019, https://www.thoughtco.com/banana-republic-definition-4776041.

10 Mary Gormandy White, "What Is a Banana Republic? Explanation and Examples," Your Dictionary, last updated August 23, 2022, https://www.yourdictionary.com/articles/banana-republic-explained.

- Widespread government corruption [Guilty]
- Tyrannical government [Guilty]
- Unstable government [Guilty]
- Civil unrest [Guilty]
- Coup attempts/insurgency [Guilty]
- Economic dependency on exporting a limited natural resource (which may or may not be bananas) [Guilty]
- Infrastructure owned/supported by out-of-country interests [Guilty]
- Overall economic dependency on foreign investment or business entities [Guilty]
- Widespread poverty [Guilty]
- Significant stratification of social classes [Guilty]
- Enormous gap between the haves and have nots [Guilty]
- Lack of a middle class [going, going . . .]

After viewing this list and understanding the current condition of America, one might ask the obvious question, "How did we move so quickly away from a constitutional republic, where the rule of law is supreme, to becoming a Banana Republic, where the power of a thug dictator is supreme?"

Was it ignorance or intent? What do you think? Now ask yourself, "Who am I following, and why?" Is this what you really desire? You haven't been fooled, have you?

HYPOCRITICAL LOVE OR GENUINE CONCERN

One thing I can say about charlatan and huckster politicians is this, "They care about your vote, but not about you!" Is that not obvious to you? If not yet, it will be soon!

The kind of love that God had for man is "agape" love. It means to sacrifice oneself for the benefit of the other. This is only done because there is an authentic concern and a genuine love.

When you consider the political leaders you are following today at the local, state, and federal levels, have you ever asked yourself, "What are they sacrificing and what is the benefit to me, my family, and our community?" May I suggest to you that you run your loyalty through the filter of that question? (WARNING: You may be surprised at what you determine.) Fear not, my friend, the discovery you make. The truth always wins! You can deny God and his Word, but neither will change! You will lose your battle of rejection!

STIRRING YOU TO DESTROY YOU

One of the methods that has been used over the last half century is a perversion of community activism. Once considered a good or favorable initiative conducted by honest, compassionate people, community activism today has morphed from "organization" into "agitation," the sinister stirring one group up against another group. We may think this is often accomplished by thugs with masks and hoods covering their face and hands filled with weapons of destruction. But just like the professor in the *Wizard of Oz*, their leaders are the charlatans who are standing behind their curtain, shouting into their microphones with a deep, feigned voices projecting power, "disregard that little man behind the curtain."

For decades, the Democratic party has aligned itself

with groups like Antifa, Black Lives Matter, the Black Panthers, Defund the Police, Earth Liberation Front, and other terrorist organizations and have employed their evil strategies to advance their secret agendas. Have you noticed that the rule of the day for the progressive Left has become violent protest? Create chaos and crisis, and then don't let a good crisis go to waste! Are you even aware that many of the elected Democrat leaders in the 2020 presidential election cycle provided financial support to these rebel groups? The Democrat Senate majority leader, Chuck Schumer, stood on the Supreme Court's steps and illegally threatened our Supreme Court justices with violence and destruction. He had no intention of doing the violence himself, instead, he delegated it to his activist allies. Do you see the clever strategy? Not long after this, a zealot was arrested near Justice Brett Kavanaugh's home armed with weapons and intent to kill him and his family.[11] You might respond to this by saying "I don't believe it!" Well, okay! But do not remain ignorant, or should I say willingly ignorant. Look for yourself.

STAND UP; OR SIT DOWN AND SHUT UP

America needs a true champion—a statesman, not a politician! A true statesman puts the country's welfare first, not a personal or political party agenda. They are rare and difficult to find! I have only seen a few in my lifetime.

---

11 Mark Sherman, Michael Balsamo, and Michael Kunzelman, "Armed Man Arrested for Threat to Kill Justice Kavanaugh," AP News, June 8, 2022, https://apnews.com/article/us-supreme-court-brett-kavanaugh-district-of-columbia-maryland-government-and-politics-179d18e7f933b3decbaddb-542ceb0b29.

There are few, if any, examples in history of a person "speaking truth to power" that are more compelling than Moses speaking truth to Pharaoh, the leader of the known world approximately 3,300 years ago. While it may be difficult for us to visualize the scene or to understand the tension of the moment or the sense of fear that was likely to present in Moses' heart, we do know that Moses was being driven by his desire to obey his Lord's command.

After decades of a quiet life of solitude on the backside of a desert in Midian, God told Moses to go back to Egypt, the very land he had fled while fearing for his own life 40 years earlier. He was sent by his Master, not to protest his own opinions and feelings, rather, to deliver a stern message from the Creator of the universe to the most powerful man on earth at that time. "Let my people go!" Not driven by politics, with no fear of the opinions of his peers, with no desire or intent for personal gain, willing to risk his life, fortune, and sacred honor, Moses stood up and spoke truth to power.

I considered Ronald Reagan a statesman. A humble Hollywood actor with a boatload of common sense and a deep loyalty to the American Idea and the Constitution. He sacrificed a successful career in film, alienating himself from many of his Hollywood friends, to take on the risk of helping his state, California, and then his country, the United States of America. He was rich for sure. He is one of those people who "became rich and then went to Washington." It would not be wrong for anyone to think of Reagan as "pledging and risking his life, his fortune, and his sacred honor" and doing so for the benefit of his country and its people. You may want those you follow or

91

adore to take this same test. Would they make the pledge? Would they take the risk? Have they? Did they? Will they?

Reagan was a man of moral conviction and great courage. Many have drawn hope and courage from his confrontation with the Soviet leader Mikhail Gorbachev (leader of the Soviet Union, considered one of the most dangerous superpowers of the age), when Reagan proclaimed while standing at the Berlin Wall, near the Brandenburg Gate, Friday, June 12, 1987, "*Mr. Gorbachev—tear down this wall.*" With respect and resolve, Reagan spoke truth to power. That one line altered the course of history for billions of people!

Winston Churchill is considered by some as the greatest statesman of the twentieth century. He was "the lion who roared when the British Empire needed him most." He spoke truth to power. One of my favorite quotes of his is this: "All the greatest things are simple, and many can be expressed in a single word: freedom, justice, honor, duty, mercy, hope."

I believe history will record Donald Trump as one of history's greatest statesmen. Although his run is not over yet, he has already demonstrated his love and loyalty to America in a way that far exceeds most. He was one of the most successful presidents in the history of the United States, leading an economic recovery unparalleled in history and a patriotic revival unseen for decades, even centuries.

His presidency faced more opposition than perhaps any presidency in history. His opposition, however, was unique in that it did not only come from outside the camp by a hostile foreign adversary, but it also came from inside the camp from a corrupt conspiracy of selfish, power hungry, greed-driven, politicians who bore no resemblance to a patriot! A deeply entrenched administrative state led by a conspiracy of money-hungry men and women who have no respect for our founding fathers, principles, or documents, and no regard for the truth—God's truth. This cadre of wickedness has driven a nonstop onslaught of criminal behavior that has diminished our nation's standing around the world and destroyed the faith of many of its citizens. Their philosophy of division and victimhood, disdain for freedom, and hatred for the American experiment has become obvious to most. It should be to all!

Like Reagan, Trump got rich and then went to Washington. The leaders of his opposition, with names such as Clinton, Obama, Biden, Schumer, Pelosi, Schiff, and others seemed to have "gone to Washington and got rich"! That should speak volumes to any sane person who was paying the least bit of attention to what was happening with their country. What do you think of this? Now, we have found out that poor old Joe wasn't so poor after all. Some believed his self-proclaimed poverty, and others believed the lies told by a couple vacating the premises, that their followers could empathize and would even sympathize with their need for silverware and dishes. Their love for the Clintons might even produce a vote to "return to the people's house." (Was he just whispering to her, "Gotcha Sucker"?) A subversive love of socialism and willingness to entertain Communism seems to fuel their efforts.

The Lord Jesus Christ, the conquering King of heaven, rebuked an apathetic church in Laodicea 2,000 years ago: He told his Apostle John to write the following:

And unto the angel of the church of the Laodiceans write; These things saith the Amen, the faithful and true witness, the beginning of the creation of God; I know thy works, that thou art neither cold nor hot: I would thou wert cold or hot. So then because thou art lukewarm, and neither cold nor hot, I will spue thee out of my mouth. Because thou sayest, I am rich, and increased with goods, and have need of nothing; and knowest not that thou art wretched, and miserable, and poor, and blind, and naked: I counsel thee to buy of me gold tried in the fire, that thou mayest be rich; and white raiment, that thou mayest be clothed, and that the shame of thy nakedness do not appear; and anoint thine eyes with eyesalve, that thou mayest see. As many as I love, I rebuke and chasten: be zealous therefore, and repent. Behold, I stand at the door, and knock: if any man hear my voice, and open the door, I will come in to him, and will sup with him, and he with me. To him that overcometh will I grant to sit with me in my throne, even as I also overcame, and am set down with my Father in his throne. Revelation 3:14–21

Jesus rebuked them for their lukewarmness. In much the same way, our Republican conservative elected representatives, even those known as "Rhinos," need to be exhorted to abandon their lukewarmness and engage in the battle. They were sent to the front lines to fight, not fellowship! Fellowship requires agreement, and as much as you might desire to have it, you will not find it in your political adversaries. Not now, not ever! If you are not willing to fight, and you really do believe in your heart (not in your political ads) that there are no others willing to stand, then sit down, shut up, and send a statesman back to Washington.

One more thing to address before we move on—many of our right-wing friends and pundits often voice their admiration of the "unity of the Democratic party." They have it together, always voting in a single block. In the same breath, the so-called conservative voices whine and complain that the Republicans keep failing in this same area. Stop being an idiot! There is one issue that causes all of this, on both sides of the aisle. What is it? Do you know? It is the independent thinking of people with integrity! The Democrat unity is the result of no integrity. The leadership just leads the followers around by the nose telling them what to do. They are not at liberty to think for themselves. Just do what I say! Or else! And they have certainly proven the "or else" can be severe.

Only through independent thinking and respectful debate will America find its way back home! Consider the following:

> *Honesty is the best policy* means that it is better to tell the truth than to tell a lie, no matter the consequences. Sometimes it is difficult to tell someone the truth because of the possible repercussions from telling that truth. Someone may think less of you if you tell the truth, you may lose a business deal, or you may even incur a fine or jail sentence. The proverb *honesty is the best policy* means it is better

to admit one's shortcomings and simply endure the consequences rather than live inauthentically or in fear of being found out. It is important to be honest and trustworthy and to demonstrate sincerity and truthfulness.[12]

King Solomon knew the importance of integrity and taught it to his son: "The integrity of the upright shall guide them: but the perverseness of transgressors shall destroy them" (Proverbs 11:3). Integrity is a big issue. If you don't seek integrity in a leader, you are a person of low integrity!

---

12 Grammarist Proverb, "Honesty Is the Best Policy," Grammarist, accessed November 26, 2023, https://grammarist.com/proverb/honesty-is-the-best-policy/#:~:text=The%20proverb%20honesty%20is%20the,to%20demonstrate%20sincerity%20and%20truthfulness.

CHAPTER 4
CRYBABIES AND WHINERS

I know, I know: "Sticks and stones may break my bones, but names (or words) will never hurt me." I remember, as a child, the shame of being called a "crybaby." In addition to humiliating me then, it later became obvious that someone was trying to silence me.

Whiners are rarely winners, and winners rarely whine! The weapons of a whiner are words (Words, just like the false prophets of Peter's day. Hmm . . . is there a pattern here?). All talk, no action. You must act, you must engage, and you must fight if you intend to win! You do intend to win with truth and principle, don't you?

There is an old saying that goes like this: "Your walk talks, and your talk talks, but your walk talks louder than your talk talks." For the low-information voters who may hear someone else say this, it simply means that "what you do means more than what you say."

TIRED OF HEARING "TWO-TIERED JUSTICE"

Okay, we heard from you. In fact, we keep hearing from

you, night after night on the same talk shows and our favorite news broadcasts. You restate our complaints and frustrations, and then instead of acting to facilitate change, you deflect by decrying the two-tiered justice system again and again. How about doing something to correct it? Makes me wonder if just participating in an interview is a delightful experience for politicians and the brainless hive-minders. We know there is a two-tiered system of justice! It is as plain as the nose on your face.

Instead of continuing to listen to their whining, let us be reminded that the primary role of government is not to prefer either party but to provide for "the common defense." (Stop and listen! Do you hear the hissing and booing from DC, oh that pesky Constitution again!) As a combat veteran of the war in Vietnam, I have firsthand experience in what "providing for the common defense" looks like. Unfortunately, in that war, the government of our nation failed us. They "tied the hands" of the military and altered their mission. Instead of pursuing swift and total victory by using all resources available, including our superior weaponry, air dominance, and the best-trained warriors on the planet, the political hacks redirected the military into a "likely to fail" social service mission.

The theatre motto when I was in Vietnam was this: "**Operation Pacification**." We were to "win the hearts and minds of the people"! What? Really? So what do you want us to do with the months of intense and vigorous training we have endured? Why did we spend hours on the shooting ranges? Why did we practice tossing grenades and deploying the gas masks? Why all the fitness and body sculpting? So what do you want us to do now that we are in a war zone and drawing combat pay? Did you just want us to smile at the people? Wish them well? To hand out chocolate bars and cigarettes? Are you kidding me? What about "**win the war**"? Political agendas trumped the effort to "provide for the common defense." (Did you get the pun?)

Looking back on this many years later helped me to understand a sobering truth, **the politician's profit is in the process not the product**. The outcome is not their primary concern or even a goal. They personally benefit from the process in the form of power and financial profit through exposure and vain oratory. That is their agenda! What a dirty little secret! Disgusting! No wonder we are a nation in decline. As one candidate stated recently, "The leadership has gone to hell." It does appear that they have joined the forces of hell! Maybe that is where they should go! Only by God's mercy and grace do any of us avoid that awful fate!

DO NOT ACT WHEN THEY COULD

I keep hearing our Republican leaders say that the only power we have in government is "the power of the purse." It seems they use that excuse most often when they are confronted about their inaction to issues that require action! If you have the power, then use it! Stop making excuses and stop procrastinating. Kick your reluctance to the curb and pick up a to-go box of courage! We the people are sick of the gutless practice of passing the buck or running out the clock. Do what you can! Do all you can! We understand it is a war! You may not prevail in every skirmish, but please, get on to the business of winning. Focus and fight like your life depends on it. I know what that means, and I know what that is like. It can be hard, unpleasant, discouraging, and downright terrifying. In case you did not know, or perhaps you have forgotten, there is a difference between a playground and a battlefield. On one, it is the toys and delightful activities that rule the day, on the other, bombs, blood, and death are ever present! Do you see the difference?

You never see the football fans in the stands scoring touchdowns in a Sunday afternoon game in the NFL. The fans are not the players or participants, they are fans and observers. Your fans have observed you back home, and they believed in you, you convinced them, and so they sent you to your political office to participate—but not just participate, to WIN! We are not happy that you are engaged in the process and that seems to be enough for you. That is not the goal we desired when we sent you to play the game. We want WINS! Use all the tools you have available, but WIN! Should we find you passing out chocolate bars and taking selfies with the fans in the stands or running off to the makeup room for your next prime time appearance, you will be coming home for good!

TAKE OFF THE MASK AND GET OUT

If you cannot or will not, fulfill your oath to office, then "take off the mask!" Get out! Get back in the Trojan horse you rode in on, chuck your selfish agenda, and go back to the confines of your political office! Once there, do the honorable thing—take off your mask and resign! Go home!

From the website of the United States Senate, we understand that the president and members of Congress take an oath at the beginning of their term of service by which they are bound (Bound? Some may think that means only if someone holds them accountable. Not only can they not define personal integrity or character, but they have also never heard of it!). The site informs us:[1]

> At the start of each new Congress, in January of every odd-numbered year, one-third of senators take the oath of office to begin their new terms. While the oath-taking practice dates back to the First Congress in 1789, the current oath is a product of the 1860s, drafted during the Civil War.
>
> The Constitution contains an oath of office for the president of the United States. For other officials, including members of Congress, that document specifies only that they "shall be bound by Oath or Affirmation to support this constitution." In 1789 the First Congress adopted a simple oath: "*I do solemnly swear (or affirm) that I will support the Constitution of the United States.*" [emphasis mine]
>
> The full oath as given by the website:
>
> *I do solemnly swear (or affirm) that I will support and defend the Constitution of the United States against all enemies, foreign and domestic; that I will bear true faith and allegiance to the same; that I take this*

---

1 United States Senate, "About the Senate & the U.S. Constitution," The Senate & the Constitution, accessed November 26, 2023, https://www.senate.gov/about/origins-foundations/senate-and-constitution/oath-of-office.htm.

obligation freely, without any mental reserva-
tion or purpose of evasion; and that I will well
and faithfully discharge the duties of the office
on which I am about to enter. So help me God.

The website for the Supreme Court provides the following information:[2]

Justices of the Supreme Court of the United States
are required to take two oaths before they may execute the duties of their appointed office.

The Constitutional Oath

As noted below in Article VI, all federal officials
must take an oath in support of the Constitution:
"The Senators and Representatives before
mentioned, and the Members of the several
State Legislatures, and all executive and judi-
cial Officers, both of the United States and of
the several States, shall be bound by Oath or
Affirmation, to support this Constitution;
but no religious Test shall ever be required
as a Qualification to any Office or public Trust
under the United States."

The Constitution does not provide the wording for
this oath, leaving that to the determination of Congress. From 1789 until 1861, this oath was, *"I do*
solemnly swear (or affirm) that I will support
the Constitution of the United States." During

---

2 Supreme Court of the United States, "Oaths of Office," About the Court,
accessed November 26, 2023, https://www.supremecourt.gov/about/
oath/oathsofoffice.aspx#:~:text=oaths%2C%20which%20reads%3A-
,%E2%80%9CI%2C%20_____%2C%20do%20solemnly%20
swear%20(or%20affirm),of%20the%20United%20States%3B%20and.

the 1860s, this oath was altered several times before Congress settled on the text used today, which is set out at 5 U. S. C. § 3331. This oath is now taken by all federal employees, other than the President. [emphasis mine]

The Judicial Oath

The origin of the second oath is found in the Judiciary Act of 1789, which reads "the justices of the Supreme Court, and the district judges, before they proceed to execute the duties of their respective offices" to take a second oath or affirmation. From 1789 to 1990, the original text used for this oath (1 Stat. 76 § 8) was: "*I, _____, do solemnly swear or affirm that I will administer justice without respect to persons, and do equal right to the poor and to the rich, and that I will faithfully and impartially discharge and perform all the duties incumbent upon me as _____, according to the best of my abilities and understanding, agreeably to the constitution and laws of the United States. So help me God*." [emphasis mine]

In December 1990, the Judicial Improvements Act of 1990 replaced the phrase "*according to the best of my abilities and understanding, agreeably to the Constitution*" with "*under the Constitution*." The revised Judicial Oath, found at 28 U. S. C. § 453, reads: "*I, _____, do solemnly swear (or affirm) that I will administer justice without respect to persons, and do equal right to the poor and to the rich, and that I will faithfully and impartially discharge and perform all the duties incumbent upon me as _____ under the Constitution and laws of the United States. So help me God."* [emphasis mine]

The Combined Oath

Upon occasion, appointees to the Supreme Court have taken a combined version of the two oaths, which reads: *"I, _____, do solemnly swear (or affirm) that I will administer justice without respect to persons, and do equal right to the poor and to the rich, and that I will faithfully and impartially discharge and perform all the duties incumbent upon me as _____ under the Constitution and laws of the United States; and that I will support and defend the Constitution of the United States against all enemies, foreign and domestic; that I will bear true faith and allegiance to the same; that I take this obligation freely, without any mental reservation or purpose of evasion; and that I will well and faithfully discharge the duties of the office on which I am about to enter. So help me God."*

When an elected official does not fulfill their oath and duty they should, at a minimum, be fired! They should be immediately removed from their office. It seems to me though that politicians rarely have the courage to do the right thing, right away. The voter, on the other hand, does have the power to act by going to the polls and casting an informed vote for the one who will do the right thing and would not be afraid to do it right away.

May I suggest to you to consider that "the enemy of excellent leadership is familiarity and a seared conscience." Familiarity breeds complacency. Many perceived leaders, even with the best of intentions, seem to go to Washington and get so familiar with the culture there that it breeds complacency. Their passion for truth, justice, and service to "we the people" is diminished or even destroyed as time passes. They become a follower and no longer lead. Might that be your dear congressperson?

Or maybe they go to DC determined to do right and to fix what is broken. Their perceptions are clear and their senses keen. But after so much exposure to the underbelly of the swamp dwellers, their conscience gets seared. The corruption they too once despised is no longer troubling. They learn how to compromise or cross the line just a little bit, and soon the corruption bothers them no more. Their conscience is seared! And the politician's heart begins to harden—sealed off from what is good and right. The people stop mattering, and the disease of selfishness reigns. How pathetic!

Before long, you find they are just parroting the political slogans they have learned from their newfound friends, using them to distract and deceive all who are listening. The truth is no longer a filter for what they say or what they do! Unfortunately for them, lying is no longer seen as a sin; it is a habit! And not just a bad habit, it becomes a good strategy! They have become what their constituents feared most, a political junkie! Now, instead of fighting FOR the quiet and peaceable lives of voters, they are fighting AGAINST the voters for their own well-being and enrichment. How sick must a person become before they get planted in the graveyard of corruption?

CHAPTER 5
GOODBYE AMERICA,
IT WAS NICE KNOWING YOU

I fought in Vietnam as a member of the United States Army's 82nd Airborne Division to defend and preserve freedom. My brother Gene in the US Coast Guard and my nephew Jason in the US Navy both sailed the high seas in defense of our country. My father was a marine in World War II who stormed the beaches at Guadalcanal and Rendova in the Solomon Islands. My mother was in the SPARS, supporting the same war effort. My uncle Stan was career air force who did difficult work in hard places to protect the freedoms that were so appreciated and enjoyed by his wife, his daughters, and his fellow countrymen. He was key in representing our nation in developing the way forward for our nation and the people of Japan after the atomic bombs had done their damage to Hiroshima and Nagasaki. Uncle Jim was US Navy, Cousin Eddie fought with me in the 82nd, and many others in our family have fought, and some have died to preserve the freedoms and precious gift to the world that we know as the United States of America.

And now, with tears flowing, a lump in my throat, and with my heart so heavy it is about to break, it really does seem like we are about to lose it! Honestly, I feel the hurt of betrayal like I have never experienced it before! If my hope was not in the Lord, I would have no hope at all!

CITY ON THE HILL

America was once a nation that stood head and shoulders above all the other nations on earth. In fact, "The 1630 sermon by John Winthrop is now famous mainly for its proclamation that '***we shall be as a city upon a hill***' [emphasis added]."[1] Four hundred years of history have been written since that statement was proclaimed. "Beginning in the 1970s, Ronald Reagan placed that line, from that sermon, at the center of his political career."[2] Reagan viewed America as that city, shining brightly forth to a dark world in great need of hope!

I wonder what you were thinking when you read the above quotation. Was your mind fixed on Reagan? Was your attention drawn to John Winthrop? Or, like most I would imagine, was your focus on the phrase itself, "we shall be as a city upon a hill"?

Did you ever consider that the context from which this famous quotation came was the preaching of a man of God from the Bible? The 400-year-old sermon was about the

---

1 Abram Van Engen, "How America Became 'A City Upon a Hill,'" *Humanities* 41, no.1 (Winter 2020): https://www.neh.gov/article/how-america-became-city-upon-hill#:~:text=That%201630%20sermon%20by%20John,center%20of%20his%20political%20career.

2 Engen, "How America Became."

teaching of one man who lived on earth 2,000 years ago. Jesus taught his disciples this truth in his "Sermon on the Mount." In that sermon, Jesus began by articulating the benefits to and characteristics of the true child of God. We call them the Beatitudes. The benefit to a true child of God doing the will of God was happiness, or "blessedness." Any who would understand these opening 12 verses of the sermon (Matthew 5:1–12) would truly desire them as their reality.

Then, using an earthly illustration, Jesus showed the disciple who they were to be and what their role was. They were salt and light (Matthew 5:13–14). And then Jesus elaborated on "the light":

> Ye are the light of the world. A city that is set on an hill cannot be hid. Neither do men light a candle, and put it under a bushel, but on a candlestick; and it giveth light unto all that are in the house. Let your light so shine before men, that they may see your good works, and glorify your Father which is in heaven. Matthew 5:14–16

The point that Jesus was making is this: Your life is the light of the world. You already are that because you are a true child of God. And just as a shining city on a hilltop cannot be hidden from all the other people and cities around it, your life, if you are a believer, cannot be hidden either. It should shine much like that shining city does. Anyone who understands this, which is the purpose God has for us, would not hide their life so others would not be able to see it. Jesus exhorted the disciples to "let," or allow, their lives to shine in such a way and to such a degree that everyone around them could see it.

What the people observed would be the good works

of the disciples' life. As others observed this person's life and behavior, the person would bring glory to God, not to themselves! "To glorify" means "to project an accurate opinion of something."[3] In our case, we are to project an accurate opinion or authentic picture of the person and character of Almighty God to a world lost in sin. Only when a lost sinner has an "accurate opinion of God" will they come to an understanding of their own sinfulness and turn in repentance to him and then place their faith in the finished work of the Lord Jesus Christ for salvation.

I have no doubt in my mind that America was truly that shining light once! And it could be again! But it is not right now! We are in big trouble and under constant assault. The evil nations of the world would rejoice at our demise. The saliva is dripping from their greedy, hungry fangs as they crouch in anticipation, ready to pounce at the right moment!

FRIGHTENING WORDS AND STARK REALITIES

It is a sad reality that at times in our history the government of the people, by the people, and for the people became the enemy of the people. Absolute power corrupts absolutely can be seen in no clearer way than through a tyrannical government. And there have been and are now people whose pursuit of power and fortune has placed an entire nation in great jeopardy. The enemies of our

---

3 Strong's Concordance, "Lexicon: G1392," KJV, Blue Letter Bible, accessed December 5, 2023, https://www.blueletterbible.org/lexicon/g1392/kjv/tr/0-1/.

great nation are on constant watch for moments of weakness in leadership. They view these times through the lens of opportunity. They want to displace our nation as the world's leading power by any means possible so they can move themselves into that same place.

As America's 40th president, Ronald Reagan's confidence was in God, not the country and certainly not the government of the country. He believed it was God ruling in the affairs of the country, through the service of its citizens, which was the nation's strength. He demonstrated this belief in his now famous quote: "The nine most terrifying words in the English language are: I'm from the Government, and I'm here to help."[4] Reagan clearly understood that the power of government was suspect in the minds of the people.

President Abraham Lincoln, as he addressed the nation in a time of great crisis, declared that America was the "last best hope on earth." He believed so because he knew that God was governing the affairs of men back then. If we abandon God, all hope will be lost!

Consider how the drug dealers (who are now cold-heartedly assisting in the death of more than a hundred thousand Americans every year, operating from their remote dens of seclusion) manufacture or package their drugs, head for the crowds of the city where they freely move about unnoticed, and then sell their deadly wares.

---

4 Ronald Reagan, "The President's News Conference: August 12, 1986," Ronald Reagan Presidential Foundation & Institute, accessed November 27, 2023, https://www.reaganfoundation.org/ronald-reagan/reagan-quotes-speeches/news-conference-1/.

In contrast, you may have noticed that the good people of the city who are tired of the chaos and corruption, flee to the countryside seeking goodness, peace, and serenity. If America is to continue to be that "last best hope on earth" or that "shining city on the hill," then we must attack the corruption and decay in the cities with righteous indignation. Righteousness must defeat unrighteousness. The battle is the Lord's, and he has enlisted his army of soldiers for the task. We must have the resolve to enforce the laws of the land and make the consequences of their violation more severe than any perceived benefit the perpetrator might receive by committing the crime. Refusing to "govern the people" according to the laws laid out in the Constitution is a gross violation of the enumerated powers by those who have been elected by the people. It is a failure of leadership to the detriment of all.

Solomon, considered the wisest man of his time, taught this timeless principle, "Because sentence against an evil work is not executed speedily, therefore the heart of the sons of men is fully set in them to do evil" (Ecclesiastes 8:11). It is the failure of law enforcement to apply appropriate punishment against evil behavior in a timely manner that breaks down the whole justice system. If the punishment is not worse than the crime, then the criminals will continue to commit crime. They are even emboldened to do it.

Go ahead and say it! I can already hear you. "Show me an example!" Is this really your question or is it an expression of denial? If you are struggling with honesty and reality, then just ask the CEO of Nordstrom! Ask the president of Walgreens why they have to put all their valuable items for sale in cabinets secured with locks! Ask the owner of the Wawa in Philly what he thought the reason was that 100 teenagers were ransacking his business![5] Ask the general manager of Macy's in New York or the store owners at the Magnificent Mile in downtown Chicago if they have been impacted by crime.

The elected leaders in our major cities clearly understand there is a direct link between "no consequence" and the "increase in crime." (Doesn't the sinful nature of mankind keep showing up? Huh?) Many politicians, because of their ideology, political loyalty, and bias, refuse to acknowledge the obvious. They must go! And it is only the people in those communities who can remove them. **It's the cities, stupid!**

A COMPASSIONATE APPROACH TO EFFECTIVE JUSTICE

For my entire lifetime, our nation has hosted a conflict over the issue of capital punishment, also known as the "death penalty." You may be surprised, even offended, when I tell you this: the battle over this issue is between those who love God and those who reject him. What? You might ask. Let me tell you why this is.

It was Almighty God who established human government. Following the worldwide flood and establishing a covenant with Noah to never destroy the world again by

---

5 Christine Mattson and Leah Uko, "Video: Northeast Philly Wawa Ransacked by Group of '100 Juveniles,'" Northeast Philadelphia, NBC10 Philadelphia, last updated September 26, 2022, https://www.nbcphiladelphia.com/news/local/video-northeast-philly-wawa-ransacked-by-group-of-100-juveniles/3373051/.

a flood, and confirming the covenant with the rainbow as the sign, we find the following account of God granting responsibility to participate in the governance of mankind:

> And God blessed Noah and his sons, and said unto them, Be fruitful, and multiply, and replenish the earth. And the fear of you and the dread of you shall be upon every beast of the earth, and upon every fowl of the air, upon all that moveth upon the earth, and upon all the fishes of the sea; into your hand are they delivered. Every moving thing that liveth shall be meat for you; even as the green herb have I given you all things. But flesh with the life thereof, which is the blood thereof, shall ye not eat. And surely your blood of your lives will I require; at the hand of every beast will I require it, and at the hand of man; at the hand of every man's brother will I require the life of man. ***Whoso sheddeth man's blood, by man shall his blood be shed: for in the image of God made he man.*** And you, be ye fruitful, and multiply; bring forth abundantly in the earth, and multiply therein. Genesis 9:1–7 [emphasis mine]

Simply put—if you reject capital punishment, you are rejecting the commandments, statutes, and judgements of God. Your battle is not with me, it is with God. Remember, as I told you earlier, he always wins!

So, as previously stated, unless the consequence is more severe than the action, the action will continue! Articulating the consequence when stating the law provides deterrent. For example, if congress would establish a law saying: "**If you are caught selling illicit drugs to another person in America, you will be put to death within 24 hours of being found guilty**."

Wow! Harsh you might think. But how likely would someone be to sell drugs if they understood this was the consequence? Would they engage in this evil behavior for the chance to make a few dollars? Not only would the evil behavior stop, but one would also be careful about even giving the appearance that they were engaged in this destructive action.

Sometimes compassion neuters consequence! A drug dealer is caught selling, and then, through compassion, some want to soften the consequence. While that might be merciful, it is not compassionate, especially toward the drug addict or the overdose victim. In fact, it is cruel. Why let the source continue to provide to the one who is slowly, or perhaps not so slowly, killing themselves?

True compassion comes in clear articulation of the consequence. Leave no room—no gray area—for misinterpretation. And then, the faithful, consistent, execution of the consequence should be made public as a deterrent for all who might consider engaging in the same evil work.

Is it not ironic that the "death penalty" is considered by some as cruel and unusual punishment, and yet murder (in the form of abortion), drug dealing, and other crimes that intentionally rob man of the quiet and peaceable life is not? Instead, they are tolerated, and compassion is extended to their perpetrators.

To take this one step further, in this America, this one nation under God, we the people, in order to form a more perfect union, should be compassionate to this extent:

those who are being put to death for their crimes should be given one final opportunity to hear what the will of God for them truly is. We are told the following about God in 1 Timothy 2: "Who will have all men to be saved, and to come unto the knowledge of the truth. For there is one God, and one mediator between God and men, the man Christ Jesus; Who gave himself a ransom for all, to be testified in due time." One mediator! Only one! Jesus said it quite clearly, "I am the way, the truth, and the life: no man cometh unto the Father, but by me" (John 14:6).

So here is a plan that would be highly effective in addressing our present distress. For those found guilty of a crime that carried the consequence of the death penalty, in the execution of their sentence, just before they are put to death, have an ordained minister of God's Word share the gospel of Jesus Christ with them one last time, encouraging them to take God at his Word. (Note, nothing about religion or church here. Compassion is the motive, not proselytizing.) Give them a moment to consider the opportunity and do business with God if they so choose to do. This is where justice and compassion find common ground. The condemned, like one of the thieves who were crucified beside Jesus, has the opportunity for a "deathbed conversion." It will not prolong their time on planet earth, but it will reconcile them to God and establish them for all of eternity. This opportunity fits perfectly with "one nation under God" and "in God we trust." To reject the Savior at that point would not only be the exercise of a foolish man's free will, but it would also unleash the vengeance of God Almighty, and vengeance belongs to him (1 Thessalonians 1:7–8; Hebrews 10:30). Those who are victimized of the crimes can receive justice too, as they can experience some level of closure!

You might be saying to yourself right now, "Boy, that is harsh!" It is harsh punishment for violating laws that seriously wound or kill the innocent! You know, those who have been living a quiet and peaceable life until the violent behavior of an evil criminal turned their world upside down. And then "harsh" is a highly effective deterrent. In comparison, compassion is no deterrent at all!

So what should our government do? Congress should revisit established law and perhaps amend some laws by articulating the consequence for violating the law! The president, with our military, should execute the law. If any refuses to do his job or is derelict in his duty, he should be impeached and removed from office. The judicial branch should uphold the law. They are not at liberty to change or reinterpret the law. Failure to fulfill their responsibilities should result in removal from the bench.

FAILING TO LEARN IS LEARNING TO FAIL

Remember: If there is one thing we fail to learn from history, it is that we fail to learn from history.

Alex Hassilev was a founding member of a popular music trio known as the Limeliters. Hassilev wrote the lyrics to a song the group recorded and released in the '60s as a "protest song" of the war in Vietnam. It was titled, "A Hundred Men."

The song circulated the battlefields of Vietnam and became the sentiments of many soldiers who were living the horrible realities of war. The echoes of that day have returned and are growing louder and louder every day, especially to those of us who were there. Is history about to repeat itself? I encourage you to read the lyrics to that song.

Can you imagine this scenario? A game-show host, who is incognito on the streets of the big city, walking about with his concealed microphone while his camera-man lurks in the distance, filming the host's encounters with "the man on the street." The host walks up to a man and politely asks, "**Sir, do you know what the definition of apathy is**?" The man, with a face quite uninterested, looked at the one asking the question and replied, "**I don't care**!" Upon hearing the man's response, the host began jumping up and down and shouting, "**Yes! That's right! That's right! You just won a hundred dollars**." Perplexed, the man quietly took the money, put it in his pocket, and sauntered away.

In case you missed the point, the reason people do not care is apathy! They are not interested. And with their head in the sand, and no concern for what is about to come, they can go on living this carefree existence.

During my time in the army, there was another protest song that challenged a nation's apathy. It was called "The Eve of Destruction." Consider the lyrics written by P. F. Sloan that were recorded and made popular by Barry McGuire. The music and message of that song captured the confusion, despair, hypocrisy, and contradiction of the times. I challenge you to look up the words.

McGuire seemed to capture the sentiments and cries of the younger generation of that time, as they looked to the older, more experienced generations for leadership, encouragement, and hope. The lack of response to their cries, however, turned to anger, rejection, and rebellion that ushered in a huge cultural change from which our nation has still not recovered. The turbulent '60s have proven to be one of the most volatile eras in our nation's history. With prayer in public schools banned in 1962, the nation's decline shifted into full speed. Judgment has come in the form of God letting man have his own way. And what a mess man has made of his life and country. (If you are interested in a precedent, check out 1 Samuel 8 in the Bible. There is nothing new under the sun. History repeated itself in 1962, and it is about to do so again. Stupid is as stupid does!)

I can remember my own response back then to the mixed messages of the culture. My trust in the government and media was irreparably damaged. I had already lived through the hellish relationships in our home while I was growing up, experiencing its shattering, and enduring the shame and stigma that came with the eventual divorce. For me, "the home" did not seem to have the answers to life. And I had no church experience on which to lean. The government was letting us down too. I had watched young men in my unit in Vietnam fight and die, even while they were too young to vote or legally drink a beer.

The pain and suffering of that time found no hope in family, faith, or government. And so, they turned to the euphoria and prospect of escaping from reality of life to the false hope offered by alcohol, marijuana, benzos, meth and other amphetamines, and the exotics such as LSD, magic mushrooms, and the like. Anything that would alter the mind and the mood was deemed acceptable. Talk about chaos!

And then, they would couple the drug use with the strange, erotic, mind-piercing sounds of a new genre of music. The combination was deadly! Woodstock exposed the huge moral collapse of the culture. Flesh and filth ruled the day. John Lennon was not about to let the crisis of the day pass without attempting to advance his anti-God agenda. He wrote a song that has sealed his legacy, an anthem of sorts for the sons of the '60s, called "Imagine." He too, like others before him, would use the medium of music to advance his ungodly message. Think for a moment of the appeal of his message back then, and how it still seeks followers of this ungodly philosophy. You should search the words that Lennon wrote. We are still reaping the awful harvest of the evil seeds that were sown then.

I look at Lennon, and his performance of this song, and in my mind, I see a picture. Lennon is strolling down a beautiful, peaceful path through a mature garden, with the flowers all in bloom, and as all the songbirds are singing their songs to one another, Lennon sings his song to those along the way who are living their lives carefree, unconcerned, and thinking only thoughts of bliss. Like a pied piper, his appeal is, "Join me on my way to Utopia! Together we can join the rest of the world and live there in peace forever. No fighting, no war, no pressure from your church, no consequence for sin, and no accountability to God. No thoughts or worries about tomorrow, just living for today, for your own enjoyment, with no responsibility at all. Imagine no countries, no borders, where the people come and go as they please."

His appeal is to follow him to this place where there is nothing negative, nothing stained with sin, everything is positive and "peaches and cream" every day, all day, and every night, all night. He is sending the subtle message of "put out of your mind anything other than positive thoughts!" Disregard the fact that you have a fallen nature that is a slave to sin! Reject the truth that all of our righteousness is to the Lord of heaven as filthy rags. Menstrual rags at that! Here is how Isaiah the prophet stated this truth: "But we are all as an unclean thing, and all our righteousnesses are as filthy rags; and we all do fade as a leaf; and our iniquities, like the wind, have taken us away" (Isaiah 64:6).

Lennon, in either his ignorance or with intention, was undermining the God of heaven, the Creator of heaven and earth. The youth of our nation and many adults as well clamored to him and his band, The Beatles, as though they were gods, and we welcomed them to our shores with open arms. There are certainly some lessons to be learned here, perhaps one of the greatest is this lesson: the Trojan horse is already inside the city gates of America, and the soldiers inside are intent on destroying us. If we patriots will not stand up and fill the gap in the hedge, we can begin waving goodbye! Do you care?

Please allow me to paint the scene of my reality from a half century ago: Our squad is strategically placed, laying quiet and motionless in the tree lines, covered with the natural camouflage of the jungle's foliage and our own "tiger stripe." Our eyes fixed on the dikes of the adjacent rice paddies. We believed there would be enemy activity along this route at some point during the night.

Each of us are "locked and loaded" and have some extra magazines readily available. Each magazine was filled with 20 more 5.56 mm caliber rounds for our M16A1 automatic rifles. These little ever-present companions of the soldier were effective up to 600 yards, and they could deliver deadly force at the rate of 700/800 rounds per minute. That means you could empty a magazine of twenty rounds in about one and a half seconds. There were times when that did not seem fast enough!

The night was dark, very dark. The overcast skies of the rainy season provided no means of viewing the moon or the shining stars we knew were up there somewhere. Only a slight difference between the blackness of the landscape and dimly lit sky. There was just enough light though, to see the shadowy figures of the enemy as they made their way down the dikes.

The minutes turned into hours as we waited in quiet anticipation of what might be next. Waiting in silence, waiting, waiting, and waiting. All of a sudden, we could hear the eerie, faint strumming of a guitar. As the volume increased the tune became familiar. And then the soft, appealing words from the lips of music icons Peter, Paul, and Mary, "Where Have All the Flowers Gone." This jungle serenade was eerie!

However, we knew what it was! The cycle of the verses of this song were intended to distract us from our mission and trigger the thoughts of home. Imagine yourself in that scene while you read the lyrics. The cycle of verses sent the soldiers a clear message from the enemy, "you are about to die!"

And as we lay there in stunned silence, now distracted ever so slightly, all hell breaks loose! Bullets whizzing, rockets exploding, the fragments of shattered leaves and limbs creating motion everywhere, mines inflicting their ungodly damage, men screaming out in pain, someone calling for a medic, another crying out loud, "No! No! No!" as he had just watched his buddy's life end. The radio man frantically shouted over the static-filled field radio for more air support. He was shouting out our coordinates to those who would launch the artillery from miles away. He appealed with all the passion he could muster, "We need more, and we need it right now!" The smoke was contributing to the chaos! Visibility would grow increasingly challenging as the fight was raging.

Soon someone cries out for a medivac. "Get an LZ secured!" And then we hear the whining screams of streams of bullets from friendly gunships that have arrived on the scene to support us. Soon a grenade explodes, then another! And then an artillery shell ever so close!

Suddenly, it's quiet—deathly quiet. Then the din of the battlefield begins to slowly amplify, and the squad leaders call out for the damage reports. Recovery and regrouping begin. Soon, we will be back in our compound, still trembling, privately crying with our heads hung low, and our hands cradling our faces. Our bravado has given way to honesty. Fear begins now to turn to sorrow as we realize there are fewer of us now than there had been hours earlier when we set out to establish our ambush position. Can you see what I see?

Hey Mr. Politician, was it okay with you to send your neighbor's son off to this? How much thought did you give to this when you were creating your money-grabbing agenda? How much did you pray to the God of heaven for wisdom to know what to do and the courage to do it?

Or was there party loyalty or a political event that kept you from doing the right thing? From doing the things for which the voters really wanted your help, believing you were a good, honest man? You do remember those voters who trusted that you would not let them down, don't you?

Your oath was to support the Constitution! The Constitution was intended to provide for the common defense. The common defense would affect the quiet and peaceable lives we so desire! THIS IS THE HOPE YOU ARE TAKING FROM US!

You may have discouraged many to the point that they will never vote again! You may have inflicted wounds on their lives that will impact the generations to follow. Well, I want to be very clear to you about this, so you have little doubt about my resolve. I will stand up for God and the Constitution against all adversaries, both foreign and domestic, either Democrat, Republican, or Independent, whether they are black, white, red, brown, or orange! So help me God!

Although I am sick and tired of the ungodly behavior and am weary of warfare and no longer have the physical strength or mental acumen that I once had, **I am not ready to wave "goodbye" to America**!

CHAPTER 6
WAIT! THERE IS A SOLUTION

IT'S THE CITIES, STUPID!

In the 2020 census, we learned that 42 percent of America lived in the 25 largest metro areas. Of the 329,500,000 counted Americans, 136,828,924 live in Progressive/Democrat strongholds. Yes, there is a solution. Engagement! The GOP must reopen the lines of communication and find new lines too. We must break down the barriers of hostility and ignorance! We must engage in conversation, listen to the city dwellers, and learn from them. What are their issues? What are their perceptions of us? If we are armed with the answers to these two questions, we have an open door to change voters' minds and change how the voters determine for whom to vote. But how can we do this? How can you do this?

THE PRACTICAL SOLUTION

Begin with our own evaluation and conversation of what

we perceive the problems to be. Our understanding needs an overhaul of a dose of reality. Cast aside the party politics and loyalties in favor of brutal honesty, genuine concern, and a look through the lens of compassion for the people. This must be accomplished in person. We need reality, not perception, stereotype, or propaganda. We must not take the media's word about this. Don't even give them a voice. They have proven themselves untrustworthy. An opinion from anyone with a strong bias will not serve you well.

Next, determine who the right people are with whom to engage first. The Evil Triangle of the Black Community is powerful, but are they the right people with which to begin our quest? No!

Cities are often made of a diverse group of ethnicities and neighborhoods. Every group must be included if at all possible. This will involve reaching out! Speaking truth in love is an important principle to remember here. We must engage people who want to solve the problems not capitalize on them. And that must be our goal too. As a leader with a voice, you must gather and inspire a group of followers with a voice! Can you do it?

Then, consider the possible forums in which positive engagement can happen. Forums where there is a free exchange of thought and respect for one another, where all feel they are valued and welcomed to the conversation. We may not know today where these forums might exist, but it is imperative that we find the right forums. Let's talk about it!

Once we are engaged, then all must be heard before anyone makes their pitch to solve issues. That is the way respect can be given and received. The effect of this approach will be changed attitudes. People become more open and develop a greater sense of appreciation for each other. This develops confidence and builds teamwork so you can address the political issues that are articulated and prioritized.

With a hodgepodge of ideas and ideologies present, the prospect of conflict remains high. Opposing opinions will become obvious, but they do not have to become hostile. The key at this point is to have, and make prominent, the "filter" that will guide our thoughts and move all of us toward real, lawful solutions. In this case, the Constitution is the primary filter. It was designed to be such.

I might suggest you have a list made that includes socialist and communist countries. It could include the names of countries and peoples who reject the God of heaven, you know, the one in whom we trust! Be prepared to hand it to anyone who shows themselves a hater or rejector of the Constitution. They have no business in our country. The list will provide the direction to the exit door and an invitation to go through it. Leave! You can expect some pushback. They will claim, "But this is the only home I've known." Okay then, become one of us and enjoy America as it was intended. Stop being a leech!

ARTICULATE THE PROBLEMS

With the structure peacefully formed, get ready for the skirmishes. Our patience and kindness are about to go on trial as they will be assaulted by the heat of emotions and the pain of deep hurts from the past that have had a difficult time trying to heal. Once we start articulating

127

the problems, the battles are going to be "close to home," and the defenses of excuse and denial will stand their ground. Calmness and patience will serve all of us well at this moment. Let people express themselves. It helps get the trauma out in the open where healing can take place.

The problems may be many and severe. Just watch the evening news! What you **do not** see is peaceful, wholesome, hardworking, successful people clustered in those high-rise concentration camps of major cities. In some of the communities, you find a population of mothers and children who are totally dependent on the government for all the basic needs of life. They look to Uncle Sam as a savior! In other sectors, you find men who have been stripped of their dignity and purpose, struggling to find out the fundamental meaning of life itself. There are great populations who have migrated from foreign countries who, with no other example of what America is or can be, cluster together and continue the customs of their homeland. They have heard about freedom in America, but they have no idea of what that means to them.

These dense pockets of populations can be an enormous challenge as the dwellers endure stifling crowds of people and cars, are always on edge fearing the next flash mob, and watch as the lawless, anti-authority thugs rule the streets with fear, dominate the political class, and control the school boards of the major cities. They love a good fight and will be ready to fight.

Our confidence must be in God, and our approach must be with love and authenticity. Although we may not be able to avoid a battle, we do know that the truth always wins. Do not lose sight of this eternal truth! The truth wins!

IF THEY LIE TO ME, WILL THEY LIE TO YOU?

There will be times where we feel like, "What's the use?" Getting demoralized and being frustrated happens to all of us at times. It happens to some all the time! But don't quit! Ask God for help! Take a deep breath too. Get a drink of water, if necessary, but don't abandon the fight.

Winston Churchill said, "If you're going through hell, keep going." William James, an American philosopher of centuries past said, "Act as if what you do makes a difference. It does."

I get frustrated too, when I watch people who get lied to over and over and over again, stand in support of a liar with all the confidence you think one could muster. What is wrong with them? Why do they do that? Can't they see the problem? If a person lies to me, they will lie to you. And if you think otherwise, you are lying to yourself. Honesty is a character issue. It is also a challenge to those with the evil character flaw of embracing situational ethics. Situational ethics really means "no" ethics! I heard a preacher once say, "It is never right to do wrong to get a chance to do right!"

INTEGRITY DOES MATTER

Recently, I observed Alan Dershowitz, a very famous lawyer, make a case against the indictments of Donald Trump on FOX News. He thought his own party's actions were deplorable and that this should not be happening to the former president. And then, as he was about to end the interview, he said this, "I did not vote for Trump the first two times and I won't vote for him now." He went on to explain that whoever his party's nominee is will get his vote. Even though he sees the evil plan of his fellow Democrats and agrees that it is bad behavior, the party gets his vote. I thought to myself, "You, sir, are a coward or a coconspirator!" You are part of the problem, not part of the solution.

It is powerful men who behave like this who have little or no integrity that are leading our nation to its destruction. They shift with the political breeze and are skilled at fooling people. Beware!

SIMPLE ECONOMICS

An outline of real practical policy solutions that would help restore America to its greatness by addressing some major economic problems we currently face might look like this:

1. Energy Independence—the revenue raiser! God, yes God, has blessed us with an abundance of natural resource to provide energy.

2. The Trust Funds of Social Security and Medicare— stop robbing them by borrowing from them and losing the investment growth power they should enjoy, or they will go broke. We old people will be left naked and destitute, standing out in the cold.

3. Prudent Investing for a Stable Future—with fiscal restraint and wise financial policy, we can grow our way out of many of the problems we face. It could provide economic stabilization for our nation in the midst of a world of unstable nations.

4. Butcher the Hog—stop the earmarks. You are robbing

us while looking us in the eye asking for our votes. I refer you to Senator Paul's Festivus Report previously mentioned.

5. Balance the Budget—it's not rocket science; it is basic math. Your authority ends here! There are limits! We're in charge!

6. Eliminate Waste—especially, any departments and/or agencies that are not necessary in being a federal-level agency. There are hundreds of agencies in our government that just burden the people with expensive regulation and are an enormous consumer of taxpayer money with their bloated staffs. Essential is the key word. Look again at the Constitution and see what the government is to provide and what they are to promote. (Did you hear that! Someone said, "Do not look behind the curtain. The great and powerful wizard of . . . has spoken.") Who is that joker? We should revisit the definition of "essential" to sharpen our own understanding, then use it as the filter for determining what the federal government should and should not be doing. All services that can be moved to the free markets and privatized should be considered, even health care provision.

7. Selling Property—let's have a sale! Blue light sale in aisle four! Every piece of real estate owned by the federal government should be identified and examined to determine if it should stay or go! If the government cannot give satisfactory justification for ownership, sell it! (See step eight for direction about dispersing this windfall, it will be huge, or as some might say uuuuuge!)

8. Reducing National Debt—set the taxpayer free. The

first seven items on this list will create an enormous pool of cash. No shopping sprees, now! No government handouts! No special projects for your uncle's business or your aunt's favorite cause. The money we generate with these disciplines goes toward reducing the national debt until it is completely paid off! The annual interest payments alone make up nearly 7 percent of the budgetary need, almost $400 billion. Eliminate that and you could reduce the tax burden for every man, woman, and child, by nearly $1,100 per year, every year!

Once we do this, we can create a trophy for the Congress and name it "The Dave Ramsey Award." And then we can take the checkbook away from them and tear up their credit cards! Let them use "the envelope system"! It will help them learn what their parents and schools failed to teach them. Shine the light of accountability on the annual federal budget before one dollar of the budget is spent. We the people should be able to ask our representatives to explain that which looks out of order before the money vanishes! Along with a line-item veto for the president, Congress should provide a line-item justification for every expenditure. Is the expense justified by the Constitution? (Oh no, that pesky Constitution again? We just thought the expense would be good for the children!) In our age of technology, it would be easy to post and easy to access!

NO FURTHER THAN NECESSARY

And finally, although this could be a continuation of the

above list, it needs a section of its own as it suggests a broad solution. At the heart of this proposition is that we delegate governing authority to create and execute regulation "NO FURTHER THAN NECESSARY." Remember, everything you delegate costs you both freedom and dollars. You are giving some of your freedom away in the form of power—government power. And the people and resources that are needed to fulfill what you are delegating come from tax dollars that come from you: income tax, sales tax, gas tax, road tax, and the list would go on and on.

Wait, are you in need of a lighter moment to catch your breath about now, try this: **Tax** is the name of a 7-year-old gelding and has raced from 2019 to 2023. He finished 14th in the Kentucky Derby in 2019. "He was sired by Arch out of the Giant's Causeway mare [named] **Toll**."[1] Here it is, the horse's name is **Tax,** his mother's name is **Toll**, and her mother's name was **Yell! Tax, Toll, and Yell!** Do you recognize the experience? Do you think someone else may have had the same sentiments as some of us? Or even a burr under their saddle? Oh well, on to the more serious.

The premise of freedom and liberty is that every person has the right and opportunity to choose their life pursuits and enjoy the benefits resulting from those pursuits. Inherent in this freedom is personal responsibility, and as such, they enjoy or endure the consequence of the choices they freely make. All men are created equal does not mean all people are alike, and it does not mean

---

1 Horse Racing Nation, "Tax," Horses, Horse Racing Nation, last updated March 2023, https://www.horseracingnation.com/horse/Tax.

they have the same things. It means they all have an equal opportunity to exercise their God-given rights. We might call this "self-governing." The unalienable rights are the rights that can never be forfeited, given, or taken away. They are fundamental parts of humanity and the basis for moral interactions between people (the governed) and are irrevocable.

Because no man is superhuman and all exist with limitations, man occasionally needs help from others to succeed in his pursuits. Therefore, he gives to others the responsibility of accomplishing all or part of a task and then extends authority to operate within a set of laws or guidelines. This establishes government. To prevent those who have been granted this authority and responsibility from going rogue and abusing this power, laws are put in place that hold those persons accountable for their actions and outcomes.

In the Apostle Paul's exhortation to Pastor Timothy (1 Timothy 2:1–2), he reveals the objective of government: "I exhort therefore, that, first of all, supplications, prayers, intercessions, and giving of thanks, be made for all men; For kings, and for all that are in authority; that we may lead a quiet and peaceable life in all godliness and honesty." The Constitution of the United States says it this way: "form a more perfect Union, establish Justice, insure domestic Tranquility."

To enjoy the fullness of his liberty and freedom, the individual should delegate governing responsibility and authority NO FURTHER THAN NECESSARY and then hold responsible the parties accountable regularly to whom delegation has been made. Ultimately, man is responsible before and accountable to his Creator God. Therefore, the delegation of responsibility must be made with the understanding that man is ultimately accountable to his God for his choices. His vote matters, not only to the candidates and the country, but to his Creator too.

So let us consider what this looks like in real life. We begin with self-governing. A man is responsible for his own household. He provides for it and protects it. He is responsible for raising his family, providing for his income, and paying his own living expenses. He is responsible for being a good neighbor and a good citizen. Self-governing is required. This makes life, liberty, and the pursuit of happiness possible for him, his neighbors, and community. This is a lifelong responsibility.

In his provision, he must consider current needs and future needs. He must consider and prepare for expenses for goods and services he cannot provide for himself, such as some health care needs and defense against the aggression of a hostile neighbor or nation, etc. Not everyone can be a doctor or their own surgeon! And he must be looking ahead to his old age, where his earning capacity may diminish or disappear. So he prepares for retirement through saving and investing. He prepares in advance instead of depending on others for his welfare.

The man is responsible for the training and education of the children God gives him. This would be a responsibility with which he may or may not need help. Having a school assist in his child's education may be a necessity as he may be restricted by both time and ability. So he extends the authority and responsibility to a school, governed by a local school board, or an educational co-op or tutor, to help him with this personal responsibility. He retains responsibility but gets assistance from a governing agency so long as the agency is properly "affecting their safety and happiness." The agency serves him, he does not serve the agency. He is free; he has liberty!

Within our country's governing structure there are federal, state, county or parish, and local (city, town, or village) governing bodies. In our Constitutional Republic, powers are granted to the agencies, and their operatives, elected and nonelected, who come from the people and work for the benefit of the people. "Of the people, by the people, and for the people!"

Locally, the government, funded by the taxes of the citizens, provides services that a family could not provide for themselves. This may include things like community services (i.e., utilities and sanitation), public education, safety (i.e., law enforcement, fire protection, and emergency services), building and zoning which help protect property values and preserve safe living environments, and the administrations of these community services. The people, through their elected officials, mayors, city council, etc., grant the responsibility and authority to conduct these services to "promote the general welfare." See? The elected serve the people!

Some services may require a cooperative effort between multiple localities and so county, parish, and state agencies are needed. The tasks to the benefit of the people may be large enough geographically or expense-wise that a larger cooperative effort may be needed, and so, a county or state government is established. Once again, only goods and services that require this level of governing should be granted the responsibility and authority to these agencies by the governed. Some of these may include transportation (i.e., roads, waterways, etc.), law enforcement, utilities, hospitals, and the administration of these.

On the federal level (the United States), the Constitution requires the government to "establish" justice, "provide" for the common defense, and "promote" the general welfare to "secure the blessings of liberty." Consider again the Preamble of the Constitution of the United States:

> We the People of the United States, in Order to form a more perfect Union, establish Justice, insure domestic Tranquility, provide for the common defence, promote the general Welfare, and secure the Blessings of Liberty to ourselves and our Posterity, do ordain and establish this Constitution for the United States of America.

The Constitution gives the federal government the right to "establish justice." The laws of the land are established and conflicts resulting from their violation are settled in the courts. The federal government may provide for our common defense by establishing and commanding an armed force. The force may consist of the military and some agencies fulfilling unique tasks. They may need some infrastructure to do their job well. For example, the interstate highway system was originally designed to quickly mobilize the armed forces as a national defense provision.

And it is important to note there is a difference between providing and promoting. The federal government is to "establish" justice, "provide" for the common defense, and "promote" the general welfare. It is not the job of the federal government to buy a man's groceries or provide his entertainment or birth control. The government may establish standards that promote health and protect the food chain but not provide the food. It may create laws and regulations that ensure quality health care and its availability to all. It does not provide health care. Confusion on many of these issues allows government waste to happen.[2]

And, as much as one may appreciate the arts, nostalgia, or history, the federal government could promote those things without providing for them. The people in the private sector, including groups of people with common desires, could appreciate them enough to make provision for them if they thought the value proposition was right.

Perhaps a guiding principle for local, county, state, and federal government, all funded by taxpayer dollars, should be, "**To the benefit of everyone (citizen) or no one**." Any laws established outside these boundaries begin to pit one citizen against another, fostering resentment, hostility, and greed. It erodes the whole concept of liberty and freedom. It undermines the "more perfect union." It destroys the concept of "united," ushering in a culture of division. This may even be the strategy someone adopts to advance their agenda, good or bad.

We need to be reminded or cautioned that power and money corrupt. As Lord Acton, a nineteenth century British politician said, "Absolute power corrupts absolutely." Both history and our understanding of the nature of man lead us to agree with Lord Acton.

---

2 For an example of how government waste happens, view this video: https://www.prageru.com/video/government-cant-fix-healthcare/.

If we are not diligent in our oversight or we grow complacent about requiring accountability for the performance of these government servants, we could easily lose our liberties and freedom. On one hand, the powerful could take them away; on the other hand, the careless could give them away. In either case, liberty and freedom would be gone. Election by the people to a position of responsibility and authority can cause a man to believe he has power over the people and forget that he was elected as a servant, not a lord. And the ability to tax the people can easily be abused when elected officials lose sight of their authority and responsibility. That may happen because of a selfish motive, as they see opportunity for either personal gain or to satisfy the desires of family members, donors, or lobbyists. We have all heard about pork-barrel spending. Both major political parties in America have proven to have less than stellar discipline in budgetary matters. And nepotism (favoritism toward a family member or friend) is quite common in government! It should not be acceptable to us. As we previously noticed about the political class, some people get rich and go to Washington, and others go to Washington and get rich! Which of these is true of those you voted for in the last elections?

Liberty, freedom, unity, perfection, and tranquility come from our Creator. These concepts and truths are memorialized for our understanding and use in the Declaration of Independence and the Constitution of the United States. Both documents were fashioned by a higher influence, the Almighty Creator God. They were written "that we may lead a quiet and peaceable life in all godliness and honesty"—you know, tranquility (1 Timothy 2:2)!

CHAPTER 7
THE REAL SOLUTION

As our free nation teeters on the brink of extinction, as a people, we face a crisis of historical magnitude. We need a new generation of patriots, true statesmen, who, with courage and resolve, will stand up and shout from the rooftops of America, "Never again!" **We should be crying out in repentance to the Supreme Judge of the world**, "with a firm reliance on the protection of divine Providence," because we have sinned against him. We have turned away from him and have gone our own way. And we recognize now that we have failed to fulfill his purpose for us.

And then, like the psalmist cries out, "Wilt thou not revive us again: that thy people may rejoice in thee? Shew us thy mercy, O LORD, and grant us thy salvation. I will hear what God the Lord will speak: for he will speak peace unto his people, and to his saints: but let them not turn again to folly" (Psalm 85:6–8).

While we all desire the comfort and blessing of a quiet and peaceable life, let me encourage you with this prospect. It would be amazing and incredible if our light would once again shine brightly, to once again be the hope of the world, for the benefit of all, to the glory of God. God, for his great name's sake, must be our motive!

> For ye see your calling, brethren, how that not many wise men after the flesh, not many mighty, not many noble, are called: But God hath chosen the foolish things of the world to confound the wise; and God hath chosen the weak things of the world to confound the things which are mighty; And base things of the world, and things which are despised, hath God chosen, yea, and things which are not, to bring to nought things that are: That no flesh should glory in his presence. But of him are ye in Christ Jesus, who of God is made unto us wisdom, and righteousness, and sanctification, and redemption: That, according as it is written, He that glorieth, let him glory in the Lord. 1 Corinthians 1:26–31

"Dear Lord, please help us! As our founders needed you then, we need you now!"

ABOUT THE AUTHOR

Dr. Mike Duffy and his wife of 56 years have three children together, twelve grandchildren, and four great-grandchildren. Mike's life experience is characterized by service, integrity, leadership, and accomplishment. He grew up in a home that was shattered by alcoholism when he was in elementary school. Overcoming this tragedy and trauma early in life, he has experienced productivity and success on many levels.

Mike is a combat veteran who served a tour in Vietnam with an infantry battalion of the United States Army's Eighty-Second Airborne Division. He learned early the value and reward of working hard and excelled in a corporate career for 14 years in administrative management and sales, receiving international awards at each level for outstanding achievement and accomplishment.

Mike received Jesus Christ as his personal Savior at age 31 and committed his life to Christian ministry at age 35, ministering God's Word in nearly 1,000 ministries nationally and internationally.

He has authored other books based on his life experience, including *The Tragedies and Triumphs in an Alcoholic's*

Family, *Grandpa Saw the Light*, and *The Vivid Colors of the Wounds of War*.

The following statement from Mike reveals his heart: "There is trauma and tragedy everywhere. I believe that everyone will face some adversity in life. How one responds to adversity will shape their future. People can be paralyzed, damaged, or destroyed when adversity comes, or they can use adversity as motivation for positive change. We cannot change the past, but we do not have to live there either. We must learn from the past, look toward the future, but live today. Although no one can go back and change their beginning, they can begin today to change their ending. This is what hope looks like. I love serving God and others and have found that this approach in life is the pathway to happiness.